THE COMPLETE FLOWER ARRANGER

Jane Newdick — *Ming Veevers-Carter*

CLB

CLB 3443
This edition published in 1993 by Colour Library Books
© 1993 Colour Library Books Ltd, Godalming, Surrey
Printed and bound in Singapore
All rights reserved
ISBN 1-85833-105-6

BOOK ONE

Flower Arranging

Text by JANE NEWDICK

Photography by NEIL SUTHERLAND

Contents

First Things First
pages 10-17

Special Occasions
pages 18-37

Everyday Arrangements
pages 38-59

Sweet Simplicity
pages 60-73

Clever Centrepieces
pages 74-85

Perfect Posies
pages 86-93

Beautiful Baskets
pages 94-107

Garlands and Wreaths
pages 108-115

Flowers to Last
pages 116-123

First Things First
A Practical Guide to Preparing and Conditioning Flowers

Before you begin working with flowers, there are a few practical points to be aware of. It helps if you know which are the right tools to choose and how to get the very best out of the materials that you will be using. One or two basic techniques, such as wiring dried flowers or rescuing blooms that look less than happy, are useful to know so that with a few simple skills at your fingertips you will be able to make any of the arrangements in this book.

A range of materials and tools for working with dried flowers.

Above: *Iceland poppies need boiling water to seal their stems.*

Fresh flowers will repay a little time and effort spent on their preparation with a long and colourful life in an arrangement. If you buy flowers from a good market stall or flower shop the chances are that they will have been conditioned. This means that stems will have been cleaned of foliage and re-cut, then stood in water for several hours to have a long drink. The stems on flowers bought in a bunch out of water will have dried and possibly sealed over and will need to be cut again and given a drink. Flowers picked from a garden should also be given this preparatory treatment, preferably in the evening or early morning, which are the best times of day to gather material before too much moisture has transpired from the plant. Normal soft stems should be cut at a long slant to give the largest surface area possible to absorb water. A few very large flowers, such as delphiniums and amaryllis, have hollow stems which can be packed with a small plug of damp cotton wool to help them to drink.

Some flowers and foliage have stems that need to be seared or sealed to prevent them drooping or dropping petals. Poppies are one variety that needs to have this done. Each stem should be held over a flame for a few seconds or stood in a shallow depth of boiling water for two or three minutes. Other varieties that need the heat treatment are euphorbia and some ferns.

Boiling water can also revive wilting stems of flowers such as tulips, sunflowers, gerbera and mallow. A small amount of boiling water is poured into a narrow-necked container and the flowers are stood in this until they are revived.

Above: *Always re-cut stems on a long slant.*

Any foliage that is not wanted on a stem, or that will be below water, should be removed. Submerged leaves rapidly cloud the water and make it smell and look unpleasant in a clear container. Some flowers, such as stocks and chrysanthemums, should always have stems clear of foliage that might rot.

Left: *Clear unwanted foliage from green stems.*

Many flowers and most of the foliage used in flower arranging comes from shrubby plants with strong stems which need slightly different treatment from soft-stemmed annual or herbaceous flowers. Flowers such as lilac are cut from large shrubs or small trees and their stems have bark over a solid woody stem. Preparation of this sort of material is necessary to get the best from it. The base of the stems should be cut on a slant and the bark can be scraped or peeled back a little way to expose the stem beneath. Then either split the stem by cutting a few slices upwards with sharp secateurs or a gardening knife, or hammer the bottom few centimetres with a mallet.

Once more it is important to remove unwanted leaves and small, twiggy branches that might get in the way of the rest of the arrangement or that otherwise would stand under water. Give all woody-stemmed material a good, long conditioning drink in water at room temperature and leave in a cool place until you need to use it. Some foliage can be completely submerged in water for several hours, which makes it very crisp and unlikely to wilt later. Leaves such as beech, hornbeam, and whitebeam, which you might use in a large-scale arrangement, benefit very much from this type of treatment. A large container is obviously required and a bath is usually the best place to do this conditioning.

Above left: *Stripping thorns from a rose stem.*
Above right: *Splitting the base of a woody stem with secateurs.*

Roses need much the same treatment, but if they have large or sharp thorns it is sensible to remove these before trying to arrange them. Roses bought from a flower shop will usually have been de-thorned and nowadays many varieties are thornless. It is a slow job cutting off each thorn, but you can try running a blade or special tool along the stem, rubbing off the thorns as you go. Roses can suddenly and dramatically wilt for no apparent reason, but can often be saved by re-cutting stems and standing in boiling water.

If you plan to work with dried flowers you will need a few extra materials and equipment apart from good sharp florists' scissors or secateurs. Buy some small snips or wire cutters and use these to cut stub or rose wire – do not be tempted to use your secateurs instead. A reel of fine rose wire will be needed, as well as stiff stub wire which is sold ready cut in a choice of lengths and usually by weight.

There is a wonderful range of dried flowers to buy, but you can also dry your own as well as growing your own if you have a garden. Many flowers can be easily dried by hanging bunches in a warm airy atmosphere until crisp and completely free of moisture. Certain varieties of flowers, such as larkspur and achillea, are ideal for this. Other varieties are papery dry as they are harvested and need little treatment. Some, such as helichrysum, however, have very weak stems and are best pushed onto a stiff wire that will rust into the flower and form a new stem.

Whole flower heads can also be dried in a special desiccant that preserves the shape and colour of each bloom very well, though again a wire stem will need to be attached to the flower head for arrangements.

Above: *Many types of flower can be successfully air-dried.*

A glue gun is a useful tool for working with dried flowers, especially for attaching whole seed pods or flower heads to a wreath or the edge of a basket. There is a wide choice of special foam bases in many shapes for use with dried material and apart from cones, rings and balls, you can always cut foam to any shape you choose for free form decorations.

Left: *Perfect flower heads being prepared to be dried in a desiccant.*

Above: *A looped stub wire being attached to a helichrysum head.*

Special Occasions

There are often times when flower arrangements need to be spectacular. For example you might want to decorate the house for a party or celebration, a special homecoming or anniversary, or for one of the traditional festivals that most of us celebrate at some time during the year. This is a time to be a bit more extravagant than usual and to attempt decorations on a larger scale, perhaps. It may be enough just to choose a bigger container than normal and pick flowers that are larger and more formal than general, or colour could be the key to making something showstopping without spending more money or time than you might for an everyday type of arrangement. The actual arrangements will depend on whether your celebration focuses around a dining or buffet table, or whether you are having a gathering of people standing in one room or using the whole house. Consider such points first, then plan where to put flowers for maximum impact and practicality.

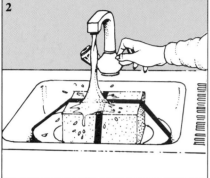

1 Tape foam to a waterproof base or plate. Use special sticky tape sold for this purpose and be sure to wrap it round and under an edge to hold foam firmly.

2 Soak the whole construction in a sink or large bucket. Follow foam manufacturers' instructions for immersion time.

3 Stand the foam in its final position and work in situ if possible, rather than trying to move the final arrangement.

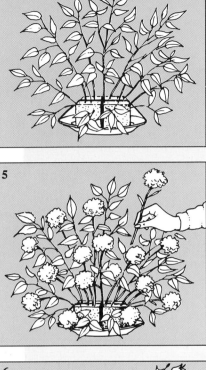

◀ *A magnificent setting such as this marble fireplace demands a lavish flower arrangement. Here the unusual colour combination of hydrangea, lilies, chillies and euphorbia makes a stunning display.*

▲ *Flowers which are to be seen from above are best arranged in situ, as in this fireplace arrangement of gerbera, lilies, irises and generous amounts of flowering shrubs and mixed foliage.*

4 Make a basic shape using foliage or stiff-stemmed shrubs or flower spikes. Bring some stems forward out from the foam almost at floor level.

5 Add any solid flower heads at this stage, distributing them evenly throughout the arrangement and keeping them within the outline shape.

6 Add lilies and arching flower sprays throughout the arrangement, filling any gaps.

21

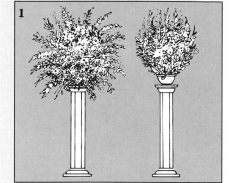

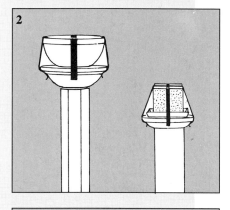

1 *Always make use of the height of a pedestal by arranging stems to curve downwards rather than in a stiff, upward outline.*

2 *Be sure to tape the container or block of foam securely to the top of the pedestal and try to keep the centre of gravity low.*

3 *There are many different styles of ready-made pedestals, both modern and old fashioned. Tall tables or plant stands work just as well, too.*

▶ *A really sumptuous but simple arrangement made using white scented* Lilium longiflorum *mixed with grey-green eucalyptus foliage and the spikey umbrella-shaped leaves of papyrus. The plain, modern white pillar looks exactly right for this style of arrangement.*

▼ *Smaller in scale but far more detailed than the two larger arrangements, this ambitious mixture of white lilac, freesias, hyacinths, chrysanthemums, ranunculus, gerbera and sprays of prunus blossom looks perfect on its pedestal, which is actually a fine antique workbox.*

◀ *Pedestal arrangements are definitely for special occasions. They can use a great deal of plant material but always look spectacular. The mechanics of the arrangement must be good and the pedestal heavy and firm so that the flowers are not likely to fall over. Gerbera, genista and antirrhinum make a superb spring mix.*

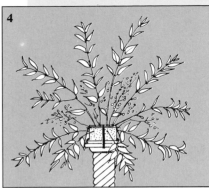

4 *Always begin a pedestal arrangement by setting the size and outline with solid shapes of foliage or filler material.*

5 *Fill in with more long-stemmed material, bringing plenty out towards the front of the arrangement.*

6 *Finally, add the important blooms and smaller material to make a balanced overall effect without empty areas.*

23

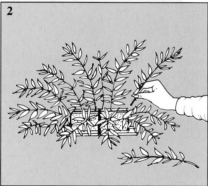

1 *Use a block or two of damp floral foam as a heavy base for the orchid arrangement. Make sure it stands on a waterproof base.*

2 *Begin with a filler of foliage to cover the foam and make a solid centre.*

3 *Work all round the foam, pushing in the stems of orchid and aiming to make a dense, low shape.*

▶ *One very effective but simple way to make a special arrangement is to use a single type of flower but in a large quantity. This always manages to look extravagant and eye-catching, but it is simple to put together. Here a long oak refectory table has been filled with a low but full arrangement of small-flowered vivid red orchids.*

▲ *The effect of a mass of white gypsophila is always light and airy and looks good set against a dark background, as here, where a large, round, polished oak table is simply adorned with a very understated arrangement contained in a round, clear glass vase. When the flowers are past their best leave them somewhere warm and dry and they will fade to a pale beige colour and, once dry, will last for many months.*

1 For an arrangement which may be top-heavy cut a square of wire mesh and crumple it to fit the neck of the vase.

2 Push the wire into the vase, leaving some of it higher than the rim. Use it alone or put it over floral foam inside the vase.

3 Put thick or woody stems through the wire mesh to keep them in place and held securely.

◀ *A cool and classic combination of white and green always looks sophisticated but fresh. It is a useful colour scheme to use in dark surroundings where many colours would simply disappear against the background. Here white honesty is put with pure white tulips.*

▶ *A fabulous mixture of dozens of different flowers is like a celebration of summer. Many of the flowers are garden grown, while others are more exotic and available only from the florist. This large-scale arrangement would make a stunning focal point in a room to be used for a party or celebration.*

▶ *A rich textural arrangement of summer flowers stands in a classic urn-shaped vase. Crumpled wire is put in the neck of the container to help support the long and top-heavy stems of larkspur, lilac, delphiniums, stocks and aquilegia.*

4 Put damp foam and crumpled wire in the vase as described. Start to add the main flowers throughout the vase.

5 Put sprays of the filler flowers amongst the main blooms. keeping them in the same plane and within the outline already set.

6 Finally, add a little extra greenery deeper into the arrangement, where it is needed, to act as a foil to the flowers.

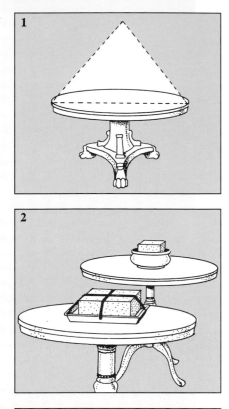

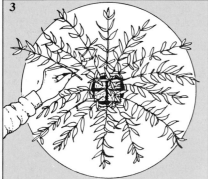

1 *Aim to fill a space with flowers which is roughly conical in shape above the top of the table.*

2 *Begin by making a good solid base from floral foam, or use a shallow container filled with foam.*

3 *Looking from above, begin with a rectangular covering of foliage stems in a circle against the table surface.*

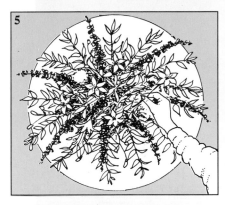

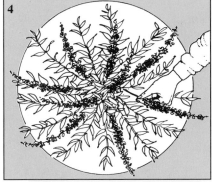

▲ Sometimes a large arrangement can be put onto a round table and designed to be viewed from all angles. This is obviously extravagant with plant material but makes a very spectacular effect for a special occasion. Here lilies, euphorbia and protea combine with richly coloured autumn foliage.

▶ A small, round pedestal table has been completely filled with an arrangement that can be viewed from all directions. A decorative vase or container isn't necessary with this type of design, where the lowest stems practically rest on the table surface.

◀ An elegant and well-proportioned hall demands a splendid, large-scale arrangement to complement it. Choose large, simple blooms which are easily seen from a distance and avoid small, fussy flowers and foliage which simply merge together.

4 Continue to fill the imaginary conical outline with foliage and then add some of the longer flowering stems.

5 Now begin to put in larger blooms and spread them throughout the arrangement to get an even effect.

6 The finished arrangement should have some stems gently curving down and maybe some breaking against the edge of the table.

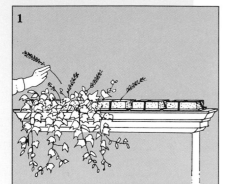

1 Stand a row of foam blocks in plastic trays along the shelf and tape them firmly in position. Cover the foam with ivy, letting some trail forward and down.

2 Add sprays of yellow mimosa and short stems of yellow chrysanthemums along the whole length of the shelf.

3 Finally, add the white irises in amongst everything else, spacing them out evenly through the yellow and green.

Decorating a mantelpiece is a superb way of making a focal point in a room. Although there is always very little space in which to create something, the flowers and foliage can be allowed to fall naturally forward to break against the edges of the mantel shelf.

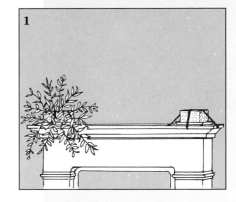

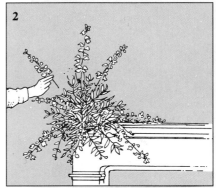

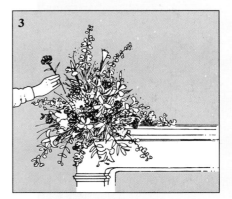

Arranging two matching flower decorations at either end of a mantelpiece leaves the picture on the wall behind unobscured. Here white irises are combined with rich red carnations and blue delphiniums in a patriotic colour scheme.

1 *Tape a block of foam on a plastic tray on each end of the mantel shelf. Begin to add foliage.*

2 *Add the long spikes of delphinium in a wheel shape and then add the white irises.*

3 *Finish of by adding the red carnations evenly spaced throughout the arrangements.*

1 *You will need, ideally, a stemmed dish or compotier. Pile with decorative fruit.*

2 *Tuck in amongst the fruit short stems of evergreen leaves in small bunches.*

3 *Finally, put short stems of roses and alstroemeria in amongst the fruit and leaves. This will last for an evening or more.*

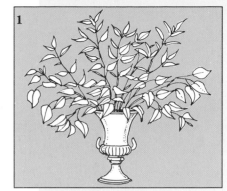

▲ *During autumn there is plenty of free material to use for flower arrangements. Look out for sprays of rosehips and branches of berries to add to the vibrant reds and oranges of garden flowers.*

◄ *In winter, when flowers are scarce, make use of glossy evergreen foliage and luscious fruit to create a spectacular table centrepiece for a party, special occasion, or during Christmas festivities.*

► *A wonderfully full and varied arrangement of summer flowers which is really only possible if you grow plenty of material in your own garden. An empty fireplace in summer needs an extravagant and beautiful way to conceal it.*

1 *Pack vase with damp foam and add crumpled wire if you wish. Put tall stems of foliage in place, fanning out the shape.*

2 *Next add the solid sedum flowers and sprays of berries and rosehips.*

3 *Finish by putting in the orange marigolds and helichrysums and three stems of pink larkspur.*

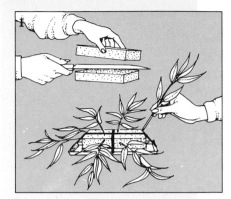

1 *For a low arrangement like this, slice a foam block in half horizontally. Soak it and put it in a waterproof tray. Begin to place the foliage.*

2 *Next put the solid flower heads in place, aiming for a regular round shape.*

3 *Lastly, place the roses throughout the arrangement, spacing them very regularly amongst the other material.*

▶ *The soft drapes of old rose-pink curtains provide a backdrop for a romantic arrangement of creamy blush roses and eucalyptus foliage for a pretty table setting for a dinner a deux.*

▼ *A wide, low arrangement of crimson amaranthus, bromeliads, eucalyptus and other exotic foliage, in startling juxtaposition to the classic furnishing and striped sofa in this elegant drawing room.*

▶ *A scheme of three separate arrangements designed to be seen as a whole makes superb use of a large, built-in storage area. The gerbera give the impact needed on such a big scale, as smaller flowers would be lost amongst so much other material.*

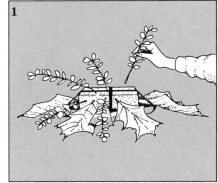

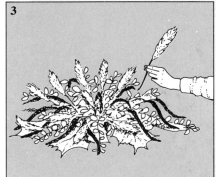

1 *Put a block of damp foam into a tray or shallow container and tape firmly. Put foliage all round the base.*

2 *Finish putting eucalyptus over foam and add amaranthus between the leaves.*

3 *Finally, put the bromeliads in place, spacing them out evenly and keeping to a low, curved outline.*

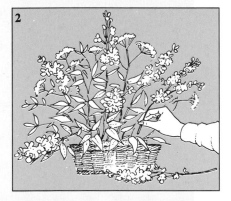

1 Line the large shallow basket with foil or plastic and wedge in damp foam to fill it. Begin to set the outline of the shape with foliage and fennel flowers.

2 Add the long stems of stocks in a fan shape, with one facing forward.

3 Now add everything else in any order. Roses, carnations, and alstroemeria should be well mixed throughout the arrangement.

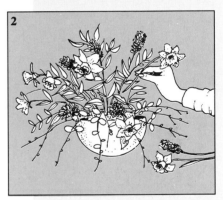

▲ *A small porcelain bowl is filled with a mixture of apricot and peach flowers to decorate a guest bedroom window sill. Several small posies or arrangements are preferable to one large one in guest rooms.*

▶ *A guest bathroom is the location for a beautiful spring bowlful of daffodils and ranunculus, hyacinths and genista. As well as ensuring that they look pretty, make flower arrangements for guests sweetly scented if possible as this is very welcoming.*

◀ *A splendid country-style arrangement in pale colours is thrown into strong relief by its background of a handsome, richly coloured woven carpet. The flowers include cream stocks, white honesty, honeysuckle, cream roses, alstroemeria and spray carnations.*

1 *Pack a small, round bowl with damp foam and begin to add sprays of foliage and genista.*

2 *Next add the hyacinth heads and daffodils, spreading them throughout the arrangement.*

3 *Lastly add the ranunculus, mixing them in amongst everything else.*

Everyday Arrangements

However busy you are, a simple arrangement or two makes a big difference to how a house looks and feels. Try to find time to put together a quick bunch of cheerful flowers for a kitchen table and something welcoming in the hall or living room. These arrangements do not need to be elaborate, but should provide a splash of colour – something fresh and alive – and if possible add the bonus of a delicious scent.

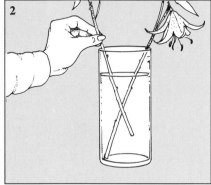

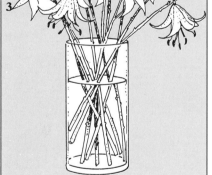

▶ *Nothing could be simpler than a tall, clear glass cylinder vase used to display several stems of the exquisite and highly scented lily Stargazer. The lilies arrange themselves as the stems fall into place.*

▼ *This apricot and blue arrangement looks quite elaborate but in fact needs no mechanics, all the stems being self-supporting. The vivid green of the early beech foliage contrasts well with pale peach roses and bluebells mixed with Queen Anne's Lace.*

1 *Cut the stems of all the lilies to the same length, keeping them as long as possible.*

2 *Start by putting just one stem in place, following this with a second one leaning the opposite way.*

3 *Continue adding the rest of the stems, crossing them to lock them into place and spreading the lilies right round the vase equally.*

▶ *An old-fashioned cream china jug makes a perfect container for a mixture of early summer flowers including sweet peas, ranunculus, honeysuckle, larkspur, anemones, bouvardia and Michaelmas daisies.*

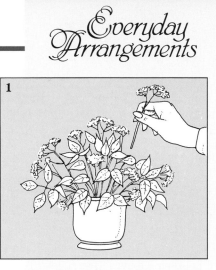

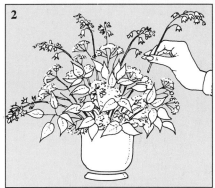

1 *Fill a vase with water. Put the stems of beech and Queen Anne's Lace in place, spreading them out evenly.*

2 *Next add bluebell stems, arranging them throughout the foliage and aiming for a full but even effect.*

3 *Finish off with roses and spray carnations, with the blooms facing toward the front of the arrangement as far as possible.*

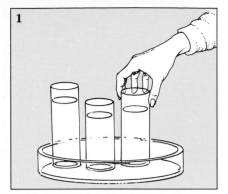

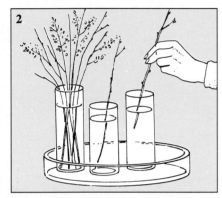

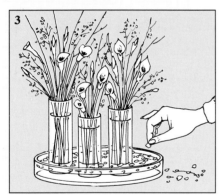

1 *Stand three clear glass cylinders or drinking glasses in a large, round shallow glass dish. Fill the glasses with water.*

2 *Put the twigs in place first, followed by the sprigs of genista, mixing them equally throughout the three containers.*

3 *Finally add the yellow calla lilies. Pour some water into the shallow round dish and float genista flowers on the surface.*

◀ *This stunning golden yellow arrangement is sophisticated but simple. Once you have the right containers and choice of flowers, it is simplicity itself to put together. The colour scheme has been very carefully chosen to work in this particular room but the idea would look equally good in pink or red.*

▶ *Peachy pink gerbera have marvellous stiff stems which stay just where you put them. Placed in a narrow-necked container they need no other mechanics and make a bold modern statement here in contrast to a pretty, florally decorated bedroom.*

▲ *Pale apricot tulips need no adornment apart from being teamed with a contrasting almond green jug. Tulips are unusual in that they continue to grow and move once picked and put in water, and this needs to be allowed for in the way that they are arranged.*

▶ *Flowers of a single variety often look best used simply and without any extra material. Here golden sunny daffodils are cut to the same length and packed quite tightly into a classic oblong glass tank container. This treatment can be used with other flowers too.*

1 *Take all the flowers in your hand and cut off the bottom of the stems to make them an equal length. Fill the tank with water.*

2 *Take all the flowers in one hand, or both if the stems are very thick.*

3 *Put the bunch into the tank of water and make sure the stems are all touching the bottom. Loosen out the flower heads if they seem to be too bunched together.*

43

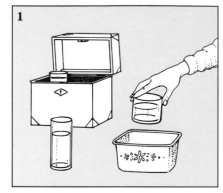

1 *Many different kinds of containers can be used to hold flowers, and even if they are not waterproof, an inner liner can be improvised.*

2 *Keep the stems of the flowers fairly long for the larger container and trim them very short for the lower dish.*

3 *Put longer-stemmed flowers in the main container and leave heads quite loose. Put the very short stemmed blooms in the dish in front.*

◄ *Unlikely objects can be pressed into service as vases as long as can you find a way to line them or conceal a container with water in it. Here a small wooden box has been filled with a mixture of garden pansies and violas which are standing in water inside glass jars hidden in the box.*

► *All kinds of unusual containers can be used to make interesting arrangements. A silver cornucopia is the perfect foil for the brilliant velvety petals of a bunch of mixed anemones. Remember that a group of two or more small arrangements can give much more visual impact than one on its own.*

◄ *A small, richly coloured arrangement for a corner or a hall table. To save on space, a small group of flowers like this can be put into a foam base rather than a proper vase or container as long as it stands in a waterproof tray to protect polished surfaces.*

1 *Stand a soaked block of floral foam in a tray or dish. Begin with any foliage and the small red dahlias.*

2 *Add alstroemeria and larger dahlia blooms, keeping a balanced shape to the whole arrangement.*

3 *Finish off with the red rose stems, spreading them evenly throughout the arrangement and facing them forward for maximum impact.*

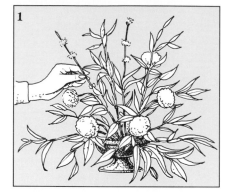

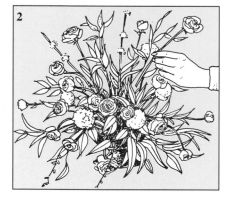

1 *Put a block of damp floral foam in a small, low vase. Put in foliage and stems of viburnum first to set the size of the arrangement.*

2 *Next add all the ranunculus, mixing them throughout the arrangement as evenly as possible and filling any gaps.*

3 *Finally add the lilies nearer the centre of the flowers and then add the large gerbera blooms, spacing them evenly.*

▶ *A very delicate and lacy mixture of blue love-in-a-mist, anemones, Queen Anne's Lace, Michaelmas daisies and rue foliage simply arranged in a stemmed glass goblet – perfect for a bedside table, dressing table or any small space.*

◀ *A neat, small-scale arrangement which would sit well on a windowsill, side table or shelf in any setting. Bright, sunny coloured ranunculus are mixed with lemon gerbera, orange lilies and pale lime green* Viburnum opulus *to dazzling effect.*

▼ *Stark simplicity comes from this modern black glass vase contrasting with the deep golden yellow of ornamental chillies, a few chrysanthemum heads and orange rosehips. A few pieces of bear grass make graphic curving lines out of the arrangement.*

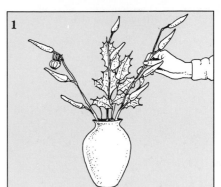

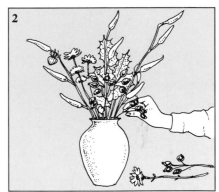

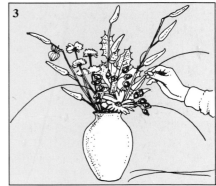

1 *Fill the vase with water, place one bold piece of foliage at the back and add the stems of chillies on either side.*

2 *Add pieces of rosehip and then the chrysanthemum sprays still within the outline set by the taller stems.*

3 *Add the final large chrysanthemum bloom and then the bear grass – one piece on one side and three on the opposite side.*

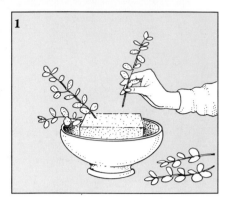

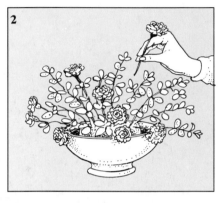

▶ *A 50s lustre bowl sponged pink with a gold rim makes just the right container for a large bunch of sugar-pink roses and paler pink spray carnations. The grey-green foliage of eucalyptus is the perfect foil.*

1 *Fill a large, round rose bowl with damp foam or crumpled wire if you prefer. Add eucalyptus leaves all over.*

2 *Next add the spray carnations throughout the foliage, working all round the bowl.*

3 *Finish by adding all the roses, filling the spaces and making a nice curved outline above the top of the bowl.*

◀ *Roses always make extravagant and beautiful arrangements. During the summer there are plenty of garden varieties to choose from but florist roses are available all the year round. Here pale shell-pink roses combine with lacy umbellifer flowers to make a charming table centrepiece.*

▶ *The miniature roses grown and sold in pots of compost for tubs and containers can easily be transplanted into containers suitable for indoor displays. Here brilliant pink roses look rustic and pretty in a bird's nest basket.*

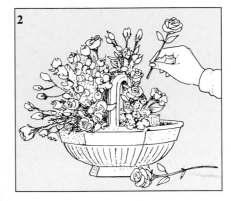

◀ *A flower-decorated pottery basket provides the colour inspiration for this small arrangement of yellow spray rosebuds, cream stock and touches of blue pulmonaria. The buds will slowly open and fill out to completely fill the basket with bloom.*

1 *Pack the container with damp foam and put the solid heads of stock in place.*

2 *Add sprays of yellow roses to completely cover the foam and to make a pleasing curving shape a little higher than the handle.*

3 *Finish off by adding touches of blue flowers in amongst the yellow.*

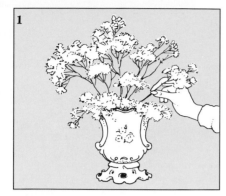

1 *Pack the vase with damp floral foam, bringing it a bit above the top of the container. Place alchemilla throughout.*

2 *Add the yellow lily and small sprays of yellow jasmine and purple geraniums, a few sweet peas or something similar.*

3 *Finish with the pink and yellow roses, letting one or two bend over. A sprig of convolvulus gives the finishing touch.*

◀ *This small arrangement takes its inspiration from the porcelain vase. The painted decoration of pink and yellow garden roses and blue convolvulus are echoed by the real flowers above. Lime green* Alchemilla mollis *makes a superb contrasting background.*

▶ *A very small and neat arrangement in an unusual colour combination of red, silver and lemon yellow which fits perfectly in the confines of a classic fireplace mantel shelf. It uses mostly garden flowers, with just a few florist's roses in deep, velvety red.*

▼ *A small, formal spring arrangement makes use of several different coloured irises available at this time of year. The foliage has been kept to a minimum and consists of long sprays of yew and the ferny leaves of rue. A few golden yellow tulips add highlights of strong colour.*

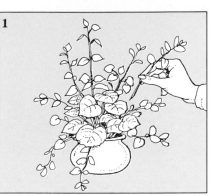

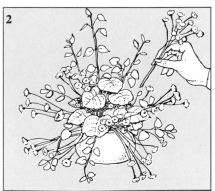

1 *Pack a small, shallow bowl with damp foam and begin to put the foliage in place.*

2 *Add the sprays of small yellow santolina button flowers, making a curving outline and facing them all towards the front.*

3 *Finally put the dahlias in place and then the rose stems, spacing them out well amongst the rest of the material.*

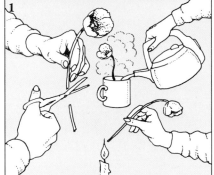

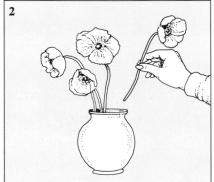

1 *Poppies need special treatment to last well in water. Cut the stem and either stand in a little boiling water for two minutes or seal over a flame.*

2 *With their large heads on very delicate stems, poppies can be difficult to arrange. Avoid foam and just stand them in water one at a time.*

3 *Mix the different colours well and let each flower find its natural position in the container.*

◀ *The simplicity and sparkling colour of Iceland poppies makes them a natural choice to use in a kitchen to add a touch of spice to the surroundings. Here they are simply put in a plain white vase and allowed to glow.*

▶ *Orange and yellow flowers give a wonderful, vibrant effect but are quite hard to arrange successfully. Here the bright orange of lilies and marigolds is tempered by plenty of white feverfew flowers and masses of green filler foliage.*

▼ *A low glass table makes a superb background for a rich mixture of burnt orange gerbera, golden lilies and sprays of euphorbia with bare winter twigs designed to be seen from above and all round.*

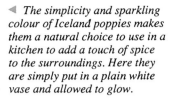

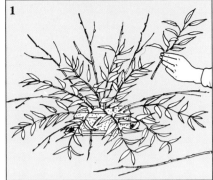

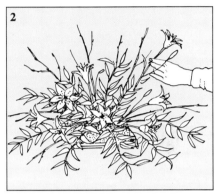

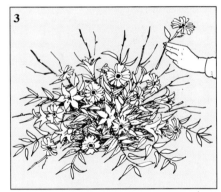

1 *Put a block of damp foam on a waterproof base and add the foliage, euphorbia and long, bare twigs.*

2 *Next add the lilies throughout the arrangement, working round in a circle.*

3 *Finally put in the gerbera daisies, grouping some of them together in a fairly natural way.*

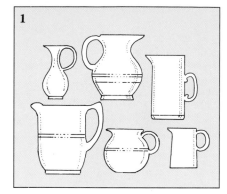

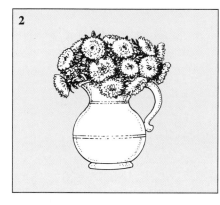

1 Jugs are useful as flower containers. They can be glass, metal or ceramic and can range from the functional to the highly decorative.

2 Informal masses of flowers look best in a jug. They hardly need to be arranged, just put into a bunch and placed in the jug.

3 Take care to get the proportion of flowers to jug right: (left) proportions good, (right) flowers too tall.

◀ A curvaceous jug suits the extravagant shapes and outlines of winter foliage. This is a mixture of variegated arum leaves, Helleborus corsicus foliage and flowers and beautifully scented hyacinths.

◀ Nearly every household has a few different jugs which can be put to use as excellent containers for all kinds of flower arrangements. Jugs always look good and seem to work with many kinds of flowers. Here bold double asters are displayed in a robust blue and cream jug.

▶ Deep coral roses and sprays of garden honeysuckle mix delightfully in a plain and simple green kitchen jug. No mechanics such as foam or wire are needed in a jug as the narrow neck holds flowers in place.

▲ A slightly more sophisticated arrangement, but the starting point was still a jug, this time an elegant, decorated one. The soft blues, mauves and greens of aquilegia, veronica and chives make a pretty arrangement for a windowsill.

1 *Fill the jug with water and start by adding stems of honeysuckle of equal length.*

2 *Next put roses of the same lengths throughout the jug, letting some flop naturally over the edge.*

3 *Finally finish off by making a small still life with just one stem of honeysuckle and a few pretty objects on the windowsill.*

▼ *A country vaseful of brilliant berries and rosehips waits to be taken indoors. The 30s vase looks superb filled with crab apples, cotoneaster berries, rosehips and bright scarlet pelargonium flowers.*

1 *Fill jug with water and put in the hydrangea flower heads and Michaelmas daisies.*

2 *Next put in the trailing vine leaves.*

3 *Finally, add the large sprays of chrysanthemums, balancing them against the weight of the hydrangeas.*

◀ *A very simple jugful of autumn flowers can be turned into something quite special by standing it in amongst a harvest festival of pumpkins and fruit and nuts. The mellow but rich colours of autumn produce are with us only briefly, but should be exploited while they are.*

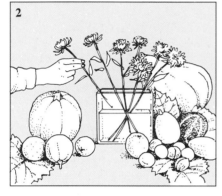

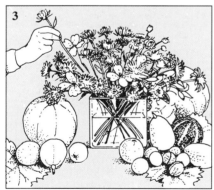

1 *Stand the tank in position and fill it with water. Put vegetables in place around tank.*

2 *Put chrysanthemums in the tank, spreading them out quite evenly.*

3 *Add helichrysums and alstroemeria and spread them throughout the arrangement. Finally re-arrange the vegetables if necessary.*

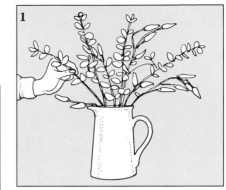

◀ *A golden arrangement to make during the autumn when garden produce is abundant. Chrysanthemums, helichrysums and alstroemeria stand simply in a plain glass tank. The gourds, nuts and pumpkins add colour and interesting shapes to the whole display.*

▶ *The simplest arrangements are often the best. Here a deep green, glossy jug holds a sunshine yellow mixture of ornamental chillies, alstroemeria, helichrysums, chrysanthemums and roses, all set off by a collection of green and yellow gourds.*

1 *Fill the jug with water and add stems of yellow chillies and eucalyptus leaves.*

2 *Add stems of alstroemeria, chrysanthemum and helichrysums amongst the foliage.*

3 *Finally, add the roses, spreading them evenly around the jug.*

Sweet Simplicity

Many people are nervous about flower arranging, imagining that there are rules to keep and styles to follow. Forget all this and go for something as simple as possible. The ideas in this chapter are perfect for modern interior or period home. What they all have is an elegance that comes from using unfussy containers and simple colour schemes. Bunches of blooms used generously, but with no complicated mechanics, will provide stunning results every time.

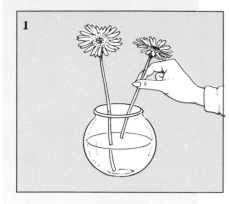

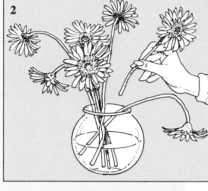

► *The strong simplicity of gerbera daisies needs boldly displaying. Try using a simple container such as this round glass gold-fish bowl and be generous in the number of blooms that you use.*

1 *Make sure that the glass bowl is clean and then fill it with water. Add blooms one at a time.*

2 *Continue to add single flowers, working round the bowl and filling the gaps. The heads will naturally turn outwards and bend over as they are quite heavy.*

3 *When you have completely filled the bowl with flowers, finish off by adding several strands of bear grass to curve away from the edge.*

◄ *Highly scented freesias are usually available all the year round and are useful for arranging with other varieties of flower as well as alone, as here, in a simple, rectangular glass vase. Keep the buds opening along the stem by removing faded and dying flowers from the bottom.*

◀ *A pretty wineglass becomes the perfect small-scale container for a simple mixture of garden flowers. The little posy is made up of honeysuckle, lily-of-the-valley, thrift, anemones and hardy geraniums all very casually arranged together.*

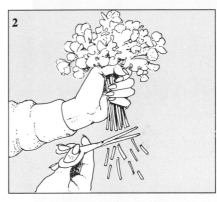

▶ *During the summer months when sweet peas are plentiful they need no other treatment than to be displayed in a plain container such as this clear glass jug. Their scent will fill the whole room and their vibrant mix of strong pastel colours always works well.*

1 *Make sure the glass jug is very clean and fill it with water. Gather up all the blooms in your hand to make a fat bunch.*

2 *Cut all the stems to the same length at whatever height is suitable for the container that you have chosen.*

3 *Still holding the flowers as a bunch, place them in the jug and let them drop. Loosen the flower heads a little if they seem to be too squashed together.*

63

1 *Begin by picking several different types of herbs. Make each type up into a small bunch of a few stems each.*

2 *Fill a jug with water and put the bunches of herbs in position.*

3 *Finish off by putting the marigolds in place round the edge of the jug and amongst the green herbs.*

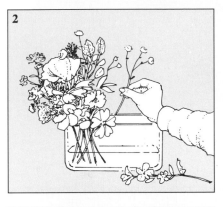

◄ *A bright kitchen windowsill is the home for a rustic pottery jug filled with decorative herbs from the garden. These include variegated mint, feverfew, brilliant orange marigolds, sage leaves, lavender and lemon balm, making a fragrant and colourful arrangement.*

▲ *Brilliant coloured early summer flowers, mainly from the garden, look at their vibrant best generously grouped in a rectangular glass tank. In this case the colour scheme is based on the fact that with flowers anything goes if you are bold enough.*

▶ *The light, papery texture of Shirley poppy petals is enhanced by the stunning colour range of the flowers. Here long stems are simply arranged in an elegant fluted goblet, silhouetted against a dark background and framed by a small cottage window.*

1 *Pick and prepare a bunch of mixed garden flowers. Remember that poppies need special treatment . Cut the stems.*

2 *Beginning at one side of the water-filled tank, put flowers in place, mixing colours and types and facing blooms towards the front.*

3 *Continue until all the flowers have been used up and you have a solid mass of blooms across the whole tank.*

65

1 Collect together a group of small bottles, or you could use glasses, tumblers or small jars.

2 Trim flower stems where necessary and put a single bloom or a bloom and leaf in the first bottle.

3 Continue putting flowers in the bottles until they are all filled and the group looks balanced and complete.

▲ *Tulips bend and grow once in water and can be difficult to arrange. It is best simply to let them do whatever they want to do, as here, and then their graceful, curving shapes are seen to advantage. The pink ranunculuses make good solid, bold shapes in contrast.*

◄ *A good and very easy way to make more of a small amount of material is to isolate each bloom and put them in their own containers. This way you create an important group with maximum effect rather than a single small bunch of mixed flowers.*

▶ *Tall-stemmed and heavy flowers such as gladioli need special treatment if they are to look good. This tall, clear glass cylinder is solid enough to keep the flowers safe and steady and shows off their handsome stems alongside a few gerberas and anemones.*

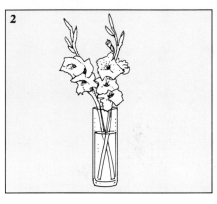

1 *Make sure that the glass container is very clean and three-quarters filled with water. Trim off all the stems, making the two gladioli about the same length.*

2 *Put the gladioli in first, with the stems leaning towards the front of the vase.*

3 *Add the gerbera daisies and anemones, filling spaces and making a neat shape.*

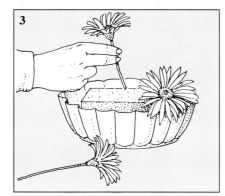

1 Search around for all kinds of different containers to inspire your flower arranging. Lots of ordinary everyday objects can easily take on a new lease of life.

2 Put a piece of damp foam into a shallow metal cake mould to hold the flowers in place.

3 Cut the stems of the gerbera quite short and push them into the foam, completely covering the whole surface and mixing the colours evenly.

▲ *Search kitchen cupboards for unlikely containers for flowers and buy a few things such as this inexpensive shiny tinned cake mould. The sparkle of the silver lifts and brightens the lovely colours of mixed gerberas cut short and arranged thickly.*

◄ *A cheerful and shiny red teapot might not be the obvious choice for a vase, but it works beautifully here with its bright arrangement of orange marigolds, mixed sweet-peas, Shirley poppies and pelargoniums all jumbled together in a riot of summer colour.*

*A flower arrangement doesn't have to be in water or foam,
but instead can consist of a group of growing plants. An old
metal hat box with a painted interior to the lid makes a perfect
container for pots of growing gerbera.*

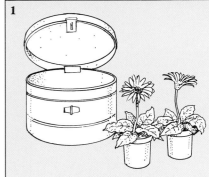

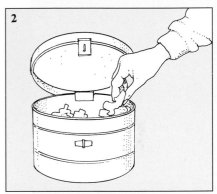

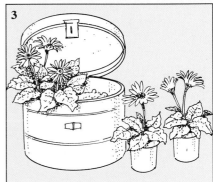

1 *Empty the box and prop the
lid open if necessary.*

2 *Put crumpled paper or plastic
in the base of the box to raise
the level of the plants.*

3 *Simply stand all the pots in
the box, mixing the various
colours and spacing the blooms
out well.*

1

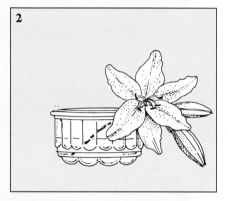

2

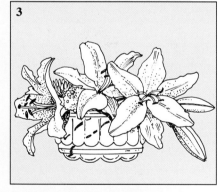

3

1 *Prepare three or four lily heads plus any buds they may have. Cut the stems quite short and do the same with the dahlia and chrysanthemum stems.*

2 *Begin by putting a lily head in place at the side of the container.*

3 *Add the rest of the lilies one by one, working across the jelly mould. Finally, add the other extra flowers you are using.*

◀ *The fabulous blooms of some scented lilies are cut short and displayed quite plainly with one or two other blooms in an interesting antique glass jelly mould. Nothing else is needed to give this arrangement any more panache.*

▶ *The minimum of effort can often produce the maximum effect. Here just four perfect dahlias and some carefully chosen foliage make a bold arrangement held in place by a handful of clear glass marbles. These are very useful items if you like to make simple flower designs.*

▶ *The simplest elements can be made into a bold and unusual arrangement. Just five gerbera blooms and a few strands of bear grass combine in a plain, round vase to stunning effect. The colour scheme, too, is controlled, which gives the whole thing even more visual strength.*

1 *Begin by gently putting a handful or two of clear glass marbles into a plain glass tank or vase. Add the water.*

2 *Put about three different bits of foliage in place. Spread them out and leave plenty of space around the leaf shapes. Use the marbles to hold the stems in place. Put in the first bloom.*

3 *Place three dahlia blooms along the front edge and one a little taller nearer the back of the vase.*

71

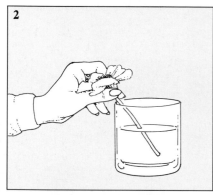

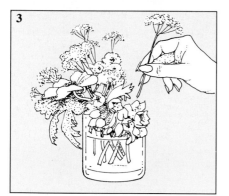

1 Clean a small tumbler and fill it with water. Collect together several different white flowers and some interesting foliage.

2 Begin with one leaf and add each piece stem by stem, building up a good mix of leaf and flower.

3 Keep adding until you have used up all the material or feel that the tumbler looks full enough.

▶ *A group of small and simple twigs, flowering shrubs and winter flowers are displayed in a collection of glasses which defines them and makes them more important than if they were massed together in one vase.*

◀ *In winter months, when flowers are so scarce, even the smallest arrangement can give the greatest pleasure. A few snowdrops picked from the garden look best displayed in a tiny container which does not detract from their fresh white and green.*

▼ *An octagonal drinking tumbler is used to hold a collection of white and green flowers and foliage including lace flower, chincherinchees, poppy seed heads and anemones. It would make a perfect decoration at a bedside or for a dining table.*

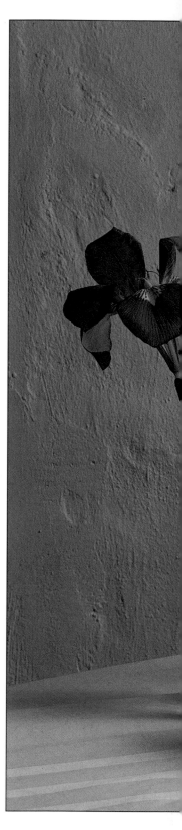

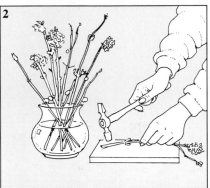

1 Collect together a group of small glasses both stemmed and plain. Fill them with water and stand them in a group.

2 Prepare any woody twigs by hammering or splitting the ends of the stems. Make small bunches of all the different garden material collected.

3 Put the small bunches of each variety into separate glasses, balancing heights and colours to make a harmonious group.

Clever Centrepieces

Good food deserves beautiful flowers to set the scene. A dining table, whether set for a quick breakfast or a leisurely dinner, looks finished and inviting with some kind of flower centrepiece. Flowers can be chosen to complement or contrast with the food, to echo a colour in plates or table linen, or simply to work within the whole room. Bear in mind that people need room to eat and to see and talk easily to other guests. Keep centrepieces fairly low and though fragrant flowers are pleasing, choose nothing too scented which might clash with the food.

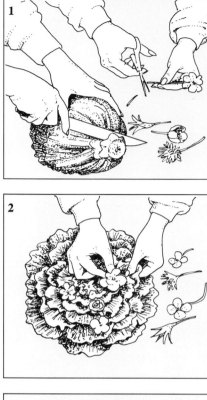

1 *Prepare the ornamental cabbage by removing any damaged or dirty outside leaves and cutting the base off the stem so that the cabbage will stand safely.*

2 *Cut the stems of the flowers quite short and tuck them in amongst the layers of leaves.*

3 *Continue adding flower heads until the cabbage looks pretty. Stand the cabbage on a plate or mat to protect the surface under it.*

◀ A decorative pink and green ornamental cabbage becomes the focus of a pretty table arrangement. As it has to last only a short time, the flowers are simply put in amongst the leaves and will look good for a few hours while the meal takes place.

▶ A prettily speckled summer squash has been hollowed out to hold a bunch of summer annuals. As long as a certain thickness of fruit is left inside the skin, a squash is quite waterproof and makes an excellent container for flowers. Stand it on a mat or plate to avoid staining precious furniture.

▼ A small golden pumpkin makes a rustic container for bright, glowing orange and yellow marigolds from the garden. Fruit and vegetables make ideal material for arrangements destined for a dining table.

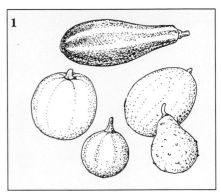

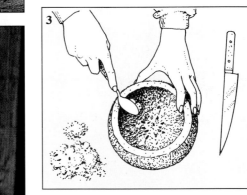

1 All kinds of small squashes, melons and pumpkins can be used as flower containers as long as they are firm and sound.

2 Take a thin slice off the bottom of the fruit so that it will stand up. Slice off the top and discard.

3 With a sharp-edged spoon, scoop out plenty of flesh, leaving enough to make a waterproof shell.

1

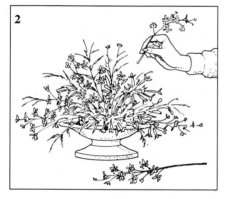

2

3

1 Tape a block of damp foam onto a shallow dish or container. Add branches of foliage all over the foam.

2 Add sprays of Michaelmas daisies and euphorbia throughout the foliage, aiming for an all round effect and regular shape.

3 Finish by putting stems of spray carnations throughout the arrangement, making sure that they are evenly distributed.

▲ *A formal dinner setting demands flowers to match. On a richly polished dining table the spray carnations and starry Michaelmas daisies are light and elegant without taking any emphasis away from gleaming glasses and sparkling cutlery.*

▶ *A sophisticated colour theme for a simple buffet meal. The madras check cloth inspires a mix of peach-coloured flowers including exotic protea, lilies, roses and chrysanthemums. The effect is casual and fun, to suit the mood of the party.*

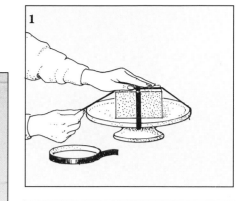

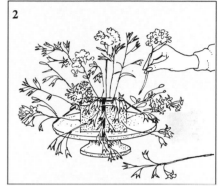

▲ *An arrangement for late summer is made using a mass of orange lilies, alstroemeria, roses, spray carnations and chrysanthemums, with branches of tiny, bright rosehips to add extra spice to the colour scheme. A perfect design for a side table or dining table.*

▶ *A classic and elegant arrangement made on a low, stemmed fruit dish. The sweetness of so much pink is counteracted by the deeper tones of the Stargazer lilies and the touches of pale blue from the drooping bells of brodiaea.*

1 *Tape a block of damp foam to a low compotier or similar dish.*

2 *Put stems of brodiaea and euphorbia in place first all over the foam.*

3 *Next put the large lily blooms in place and then finish off with the spray carnations.*

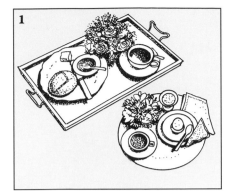

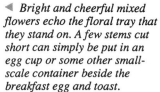

◀ *Bright and cheerful mixed flowers echo the floral tray that they stand on. A few stems cut short can simply be put in an egg cup or some other small-scale container beside the breakfast egg and toast.*

1 *Any tray, whether it is for supper by the fire or a special meal for an invalid, looks extra special with flowers added.*

2 *The simplest arrangement for a tray is a small bunch made in the hand and put into a container which will not take up too much room.*

3 *Alternatively, a small arrangement of dried flowers can be put into a foam base to decorate a tray.*

▶ *Supper by the fire and a tiny arrangement of poppy seed heads, euonymus berries, polygonum spikes and alstroemeria make a carefully chosen decoration for the tray.*

▶ *A healthy breakfast on a tray looks even more appetising with a pretty winter posy of dried flowers alongside it. Here small florets of greenish hydrangea are mixed with helichrysums and dried* Alchemilla mollis *on a colour co-ordinated tray.*

▼ *Breakfast in bed is a great way to start the day, especially when it is accompanied by a posy of flowers fresh from the garden. Love-in-a-mist and pinks mixed with scented honeysuckle shows that someone really cares.*

▶ *An individual arrangement beside a table setting is charming and shows thought for a guest. It can be as simple and quick as a few stems of fragrant freesias casually arranged in a glass tumbler.*

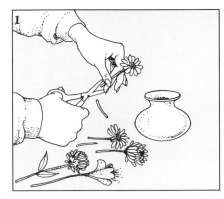

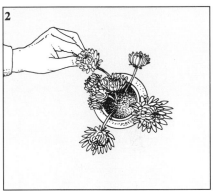

1 *Find a small container to fit the tray and fill it with water. Cut stems of flowers short enough to fit.*

2 *Put chrysanthemum heads in place first all round the container.*

3 *Next add alstroemeria and Michaelmas daisies throughout the arrangement.*

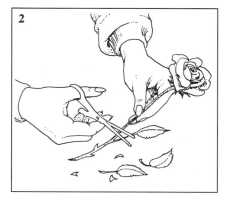

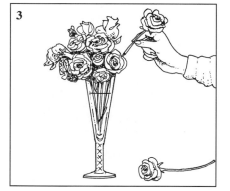

1 Clean and polish the goblet and fill with water. Collect several different types of roses.

2 Trim off the rose thorns and leaves and cut the stems at a slant.

3 Fill the goblet with roses one by one.

▲ A romantic dinner outdoors needs special flowers to complete the high summer theme. A tall glass goblet is simply filled with several different varieties of old-fashioned garden roses, richly coloured and strongly perfumed.

◄ A warm summer afternoon and a very English tea of bread and strawberry jam and strawberry tartlets is set off by a brimming basketful of garden flowers such as jasmine, roses, pelargoniums, geums and alpine strawberries.

► A simple iced sponge cake has its own flower arrangement which is designed in this case to look pretty but not to be eaten. The jugful of garden flowers combines the rich summer colour of cornflowers, sweet peas and roses.

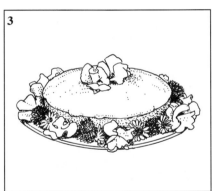

1 *Assemble a mixture of different flowers. Make sure the cake icing has set and is hard enough to put flowers on. Stand the cake on a plate with space for the flowers.*

2 *Cut the stems off the flowers leaving just the heads for the decoration of the plate.*

3 *Lay the flowers in a circle round the edge of the plate. Make a small group of flowers in the centre of the cake.*

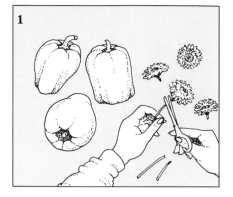

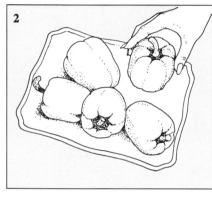

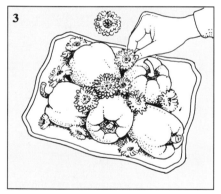

1 Choose a group of sound and fresh sweet peppers. Snip the stems off the flower heads.

2 Lay the peppers out on a shallow rectangular plate.

3 Scatter the fresh flower heads in amongst the peppers.

▶ An alfresco breakfast complete with brioche, croissants and a jug of orange juice is made even more enjoyable by a basket of brilliant, sunny coloured flowers on the green metal garden table under the vine. It hardly matters whether the sun shines or not.

◀ A tablecloth can often be the starting point or inspiration for a table arrangement. This fresh, sunny combination of acid green and yellow is highlighted by a posy of lilies, alstroemeria and chrysanthemums.

◀ A quick and simple idea for a table centrepiece is to arrange some colourful fruit or vegetables and scatter a few flower heads amongst them. Here brightly coloured sweet peppers make the base for golden yellow chrysanthemums.

◀ A simple, crisp and fresh basket of wildflowers complements an outdoor lunch. The natural colour scheme of white, yellow and green comes from a casual arrangement of buttercups and daisies.

1 *Find a waterproof container which will stand hidden in the basket. Fill the inner pot with water.*

2 *Begin to put stems of small-flowered daisies into the container and then add buttercups.*

3 *Finally add the larger white daisies evenly throughout the arrangement.*

Perfect Posies

A tiny handful of simple wild flowers or a large bunch of glamorous blooms – however you make a posy, the results are bound to please. Posies are one of the simplest ways to arrange flowers and they make an ideal gift for all kinds of occasions. Traditionally, posies are carried by a bride and her attendants and in Victorian times were given as love tokens and taken to grand balls and parties as decoration for beautiful gowns. A well-made posy can be stood in water as a ready-made flower arrangement.

1 Collect several different varieties of herb from the garden, including some that are in flower.

2 Make a posy and trim the stems to the same length. Put a rubber band round the stems to hold them in place.

3 Tie a ribbon or decorative tape around the rubber band, and if it is a gift attach a label too. Several such bunches would look good in a small basket.

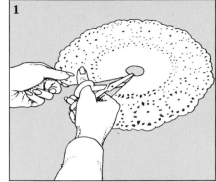

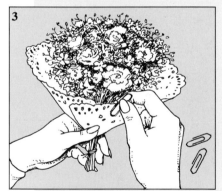

◄ *Little posies of fresh garden herbs make the most delightful gift or instant bouquet. Several bunches in a bowl in the kitchen look pretty and might provide inspiration and delicious ingredients for a keen cook. Many herbs have the bonus of pretty flowers too.*

▲ *A delightful small posy which would make a perfect arrangement for a small bridesmaid to carry. Framed by a paper lace collar, the bunch contains annual gypsophila, lime green Alchemilla mollis and Doris pinks.*

1 *Cut into the centre of a paper doiley and cut a small circle of paper out from the middle.*

2 *Make a hand-held posy of mixed flowers and tie the stems tightly in place with wire, thread or a rubber band.*

3 *Wrap the doiley around the flowers making a cone shape. Overlap the cut edges slightly and secure in place with a paperclip.*

1

2

3

1 *To make a formal Victorian-style posy of concentric rings of different colours and flowers, begin with a single central flower then add the first ring of flowers round it.*

2 *Make more rings round this using different types of flowers and/or colours. Build up circles until the posy is the right size.*

3 *Finish off the posy with a neat collar of matching leaves in a contrasting colour.*

◄ *It takes very little time and is great fun to create several very different posies from garden flowers. Years ago these little bunches were known as tussie-mussies and were carried as a protection against disease and to mask unpleasant smells.*

▼ *A bold colour scheme of yellow, white and blue which includes yellow jasmine revolutum, deep blue annual cornflowers, yellow marigolds, lavender, pale lemon achillea and the soft green seed heads of Shirley poppies. A few variegated leaves add substance.*

◄ *Deep pinks and reds combine to make a beautiful, richly coloured posy. The dusky reddish leaves of purple sage set off brilliant pelargonium flowers and spikes of polygonum. There are small fuchsia flowers too and delicate astrantia blooms like tiny pin cushions.*

▼ *Sprigs of bright green curled parsley complement the gleaming colours of kitchen garden marigolds and nasturtiums. This little posy would last surprisingly well in water and cheer up any room which needed it.*

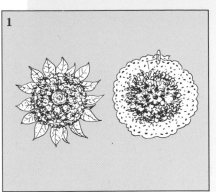

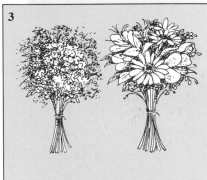

1 *Finishing touches for posies can include a paper doiley frill or collar round the edge, or any kind of decorative leaf.*

2 *Mixed posies can be simple creations with the flowers arranged at random.*

3 *You can use the basic method of making a posy to create quite large bunches. In this case use larger flowers, which show up well. Small posies demand small and dainty ingredients.*

91

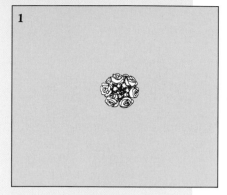

1

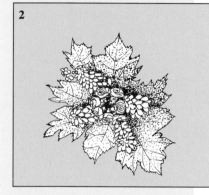

2

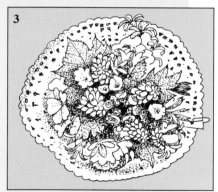

3

1 *Begin with the central flower, in this case a sprig of double perennial wallflowers.*

2 *Add a few grape hyacinths and some foliage, holding the posy in your hand and working round it.*

3 *Add primroses and other small flowers, mixing in more leaves as you go. Finally, make a paper collar and wrap it round the posy. Secure the stems tightly.*

▲ *Another posy made from spring flowers exploits the fresh colours of this season. Little clusters of blue grape hyacinths are mixed with pale yellow primroses, wallflowers, sweet violets and white pulmonaria flowers. Fresh green foliage is important to separate the different colours from each other.*

▶ *A carefully chosen mixture of flowers makes a delightful posy to give as a present. One beautiful coral rose provides the centrepiece, surrounded by deep purple sage leaves, starry London Pride, polygonum spikes, pink spray carnations and pelargonium flowers. A rich gold doiley looks splendid surrounding the posy.*

◀ *A brilliant mixture of colours combine in this posy made from spring flowers. There are purple aquilegia, yellow buttercups, pink wallflowers and variegated foliage all set off by a crisp white paper doiley collar.*

Beautiful Baskets

Baskets have always seemed a natural and highly suitable container to present flowers in. The subtle browns and beiges and interesting textures of the vast range now available, from rough and twisted to smooth and glossy, make a perfect background to the delicate petals and glowing colours of flowers and foliage. If you intend to use a basket for fresh flowers which need water then you will have to use an inner container, or take advantage of the easy-to-use floral foams, which are ideal for this particular method of display.

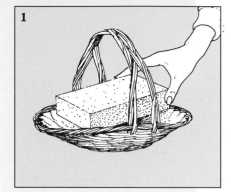

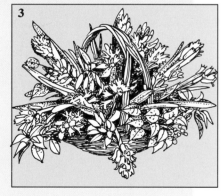

1 Put a block of damp foam to fit tightly in the lined basket.

2 Cover the foam all over with sprays of ivy, letting some hang over the edge of the basket.

3 Put a mixture of pink and white hyacinth stems throughout the ivy, aiming for an all round effect.

◀ A pretty, handled basket needs the simplest treatment to show it off best. Here pink and white hyacinths are combined generously and arranged in a mass of glossy dark green evergreen ivy leaves. The scent is soft and gentle and very evocative of spring.

▶ A fresh and simple spring arrangement full of colour and scent. The bold, dark green foliage offsets pale lemon freesias and narcissi and contrasting pink is provided by stems of hyacinths and many petalled ranunculuses, all arranged in a very casual way in a pale cane basket.

▶ An arrangement for late winter, when the first hyacinths and ranunculuses are in the flower shops and there is the start of a supply of foliage from the garden to put with them. Stems of scented viburnum and the subtle, speckled heads of hellebores add interest.

1 Put a block of damp foam in a deep, lined basket. Cover the foam with foliage.

2 Next add the stems of hyacinth evenly throughout the foliage.

3 Finally, add the stems of freesia and ranunculus, letting a few curve downwards over the edge of the basket.

1 *Pack blocks of damp foam into the lined baskets. Working on both baskets, begin by putting stems of foliage in place, tall stems at the back, short ones along the front edge.*

2 *Put the large blooms, such as hydrangeas, in place and then sprays of lace flower.*

3 *Finish by putting in stems of anemones, alstroemeria and roses.*

◄ *A pair of magnificent baskets spilling over with beautiful flowers. Using two arrangements gives an air of formality, but the flowers themselves are almost rustic. The strong shapes of sweet chestnut leaves give form and texture to the whole design.*

▼ *Using a heart-shaped basket (see overleaf) makes putting together a special Valentine's Day gift very easy. Here scented white lilac, single white daisies and apricot carnations have been arranged around golden yellow rosebuds.*

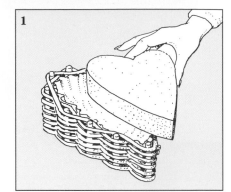

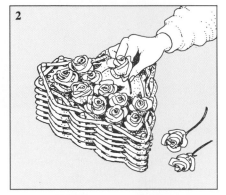

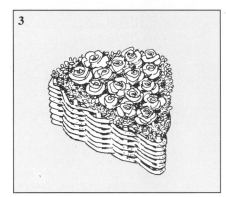

1 *Cut the foam to fit neatly into a lined basket. Soak the foam and pack it into the basket.*

2 *Put central flowers such as roses in place first, arranging them in a heart shape.*

3 *Put lilac, or whatever you are using, round the roses, completely filling the basket. No foam should show at all.*

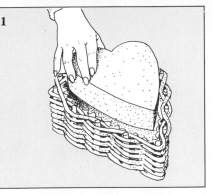

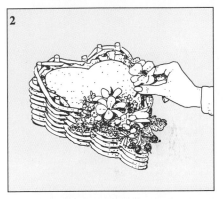

◀ *This arrangement has the feel of an old Victorian Valentine to it, and even if modern florist's roses are not scented the lilac should make up for this.*

▲ *A lot of thought has gone into the choice of flowers and colours used in this heart-shaped basket filled from the garden. Aquilegias have been combined with fluffy saxifrage, and bright pelargonium flowers sit beside soft mauve chive blooms and pale anemones.*

1 *Cut the foam to fit a lined basket. Soak the foam and pack it into place.*

2 *Using a variety of mixed flowers, push the stems into the foam, packing the flowers together closely and working across the whole area of foam.*

3 *Complete the arrangement by adding flowers all over the foam and allowing some flowers to hang slightly over the edges of the basket.*

1 Either buy a basket that is already lined, or line one of your own with strong plastic sheet.

2 Take plants from pots and put several into the basket, packing them quite close together.

3 When the basket is full of iris, push moss around their stems to completely cover the potting compost.

◀ A finely woven, glossy basket in a rich toffee brown is the perfect foil for spikes of deep purple Iris reticulata. Bought as small pot plants, they have been replanted into the lined basket and will be planted outdoors when flowering has finished.

▶ This basket arrangement of brilliant colours makes clever use of small pots of growing primroses, which can be bought readily and cheaply in late winter and early spring. They are packed quite tightly into a low, oval basket and any gaps are concealed with moss.

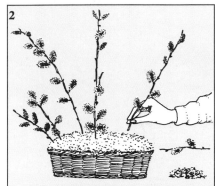

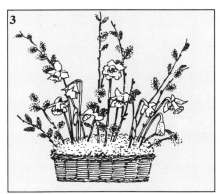

1 *Either buy a ready-lined basket or carefully line one of your own with plastic sheet. Fill the basket up to the top with damp foam.*

2 *Cover the top of the foam with fresh green moss and begin to put the first few twigs in place. Vary the height of the twigs for a natural look.*

3 *Follow up by adding stems of daffodils. Use buds and flowers, again at different heights and facing in different directions.*

103

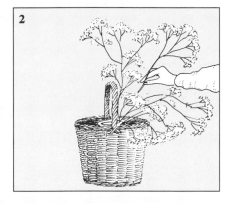

1 *Find a large, stable, waterproof container such as a glass jar which will stand hidden inside the basket. Fill it with water.*

2 *Begin to fill the jar randomly with the sprays of flowers, working all round to fill the jar and spacing the blooms out either side of the handle.*

3 *Continue filling the jar with stems until the basket looks full and generous.*

▲ *A cool white and green early-summer arrangement in a low willow basket which includes long spikes of rich green fern, soft white foxgloves, meadow grasses, white long-stemmed roses and Alchemilla mollis foliage and flowers.*

◄ *Spectacular simplicity is achieved by filling a large, pale willow shopping basket with armfuls of snowy white Queen Anne's lace (cow parsley) – a perfect solution to camouflaging an empty fireplace, or for any dark corner that needs a lift.*

▶ *A small-scale arrangement of different culinary herbs shows what a range and variety there is in their leaf colours, textures and markings. The subtle mixture includes mint, golden marjoram, fennel, rue, rosemary, feverfew, sweet woodruff, alpine strawberry and chive flowers.*

1 *For a shallow basket arrangement use damp foam to hold the flowers in place. Buy a ready-lined basket, or line it yourself with plastic or metal foil.*

2 *Work across the foam, putting stems in place starting in the middle and moving out either side. Aim for a smooth, neat, hummock-shaped outline to the flowers and foliage.*

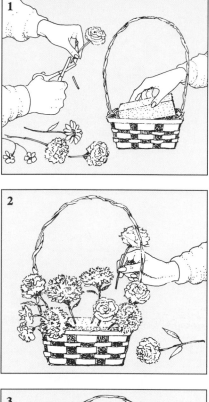

1 *Place a damp foam block in an oblong, shallow basket with a large handle. Trim the stems of a selection of flowers to short lengths.*

2 *Begin by positioning the largest blooms to create a long, low shape.*

3 *Fill in design with an even distribution of the remainder of flowers. Intersperse sprigs of gypsophila to soften the outline*

▼ *A specially designed flat basket to hold a dried flower arrangement. The flowers should be glued into place, preferably with a glue gun. Included in this mixture are roses, helichrysums, love-in-a-mist, carthamnus and glycerined leaves, in a strong colour scheme of orange and yellow.*

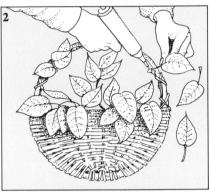

◀ *Woven stained natural wood and bright plastic combine to make a pretty basket which, filled with flowers, makes an ideal gift. The tall handle makes it easy to carry. Choose simple flowers, such as single daisies and spray carnations, to fit with the style of the basket.*

1 *Have ready a collection of dried flowers and leaves. Cut them short, leaving only a short piece of stem.*

2 *Begin by gluing leaves across the front edge and a few over the handle.*

3 *Build up the rest of the design using a mixture of other dried flowers, balancing shapes and colours amongst the whole arrangement.*

Garlands & Wreaths

In recent years we have become used to seeing garlands and wreaths at all times of the year. At one time circlets of evergreens were commonly used to decorate houses at Christmas, but now there are few occasions when wreaths and garlands would not fit in. A wreath can be made on a damp foam or moss base, or dried flowers can be attached to straw, foam or twig rings. Quick and easy wreaths can be put together on a ring of woven vine branches or just on wire alone. Imagination is the only limitation.

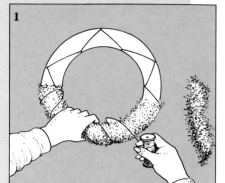

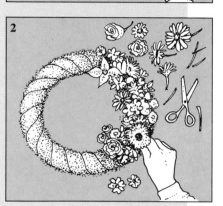

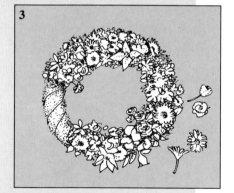

▶ *This garland was made by putting short-stemmed flowers into a damp foam wreath base. It is ideal for fresh flowers, which will last like this for several days. Lots of different species of flower have been combined to colourful effect here, including clematis, marigolds, roses, geraniums, sweet peas, geums and nasturtiums.*

1 *Begin with a wire frame. Wrap moss round the frame and wire it into place with thin rose wire.*

2 *Completely cover the frame with moss, then begin to add flowers and leaves, pushing the stems into the moss. Wire some secure if necessary.*

3 *Continue working right round the frame until it is completely covered with flowers. Spray with a mist of water to keep it fresh.*

◀ *A light and bright summer garland made from daisies, jasmine, feverfew, cornflowers, variegated mint leaves, love-in-a-mist and golden yellow achillea. Strong colours always look fresh if they are mixed with plenty of white for contrast.*

▶ *Full-flowered summer roses are the focus for this beautiful garland. To add to the fragrance, sweet peas are included too, and old-fashioned veronica and astrantia are twinned throughout the circle. It looks lovely on a mellow stone wall, but would look equally good on a door or wall indoors.*

1 *A slightly different approach to making a wreath is first to cover the frame completely with leaves or filler material.*

2 *Add single flowers of the same type at regular intervals right round the frame.*

3 *Finish by filling between main flowers with other small flowers or little bunches of blooms.*

1 Soak the foam base in a large bowl or sink. Refer to the manufacturers' instructions.

2 Cut stems short on the filler material so that you have plenty. Begin to cover the foam with the flowers.

3 Add the small flower heads and other materials, scattering them evenly throughout. Make sure the inner edges of the ring are well hidden.

◀ *This frothy wreath is made with a base of delicate* Alchemilla mollis *flowers. Tucked in amongst this are small, purple hardy geranium flowers and sweet peas. Tiny pieces of green sedum and stokesia flower heads complete the picture.*

▶ *Marigolds and nasturtiums are both culinary flowers, being used to add colour and flavour to food, particularly salads. Combined here along with* Alchemilla mollis *they make a delightful countrified garland. Golden marjoram leaves add a note of bright green and a sweet herbal scent.*

▼ *A cool and sparkling green and white garland made from late summer garden flowers. The background is steely blue rue foliage and added to this are white hydrangeas, scented jasmine, sweet peas, and veronica. Always take care when handling rue, as the juice from the stems can irritate skin that is later exposed to sunlight.*

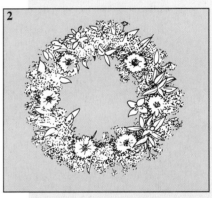

1 *Soak a foam ring base and attach a wire or some other means of hanging it later. Cover the whole ring with foliage and filler until the foam is hidden.*

2 *Add the marigold flowers throughout, spacing them evenly round the circle.*

3 *Add the nasturtiums and other smaller flowers in a more random pattern until the whole appears well balanced.*

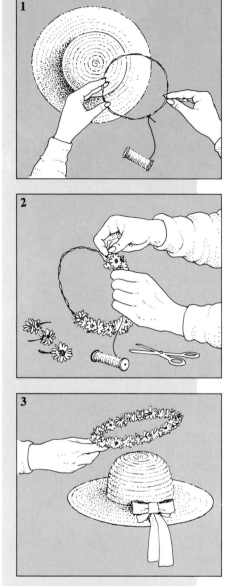

1 Make a wire circle to fit loosely over the crown of the hat. Twist the ends together and remove from hat.

2 Wire short-stemmed flower heads to the circlet, working in one direction right round the circle until you have a wreath of flowers.

3 Slide the finished ring over the hat crown and pin or wire it into place. Wire a bow in position to finish off.

◄ A child's straw hat makes a perfect base for a pretty dried flower decoration. The flowers can be wired onto a circlet around the crown, or more permanently glued into place. Here the big red bow sets off the bright helichrysums and helipterums, and adds definition and a sense of fun.

► A small-scale wreath made from dried flowers. An arrangement like this one can be created using a home-made straw base or a ready-made foam ring. Included in this version are golden yellow helichrysums, achillea flower heads and silvery sea lavender. A little deep brown foliage sets off the light colours well and the silky ribbon adds a lovely finishing touch.

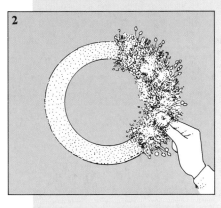

1 *You will need a dry foam ring and flower material with stems cut short. Some flowers with soft stems may need to be wired.*

2 *Begin to cover the foam ring with a base of filler material. Work all around until the ring is covered.*

3 *Add single flower heads throughout the base covering, keeping the spacing between flowers fairly even and the colours well balanced.*

Flowers to Last

Dried flowers are a wonderful way of bringing colour to a house in winter, when fresh flowers are scarce and expensive, or for rooms that are just not suitable for any other kind of decoration. Warm, centrally heated houses mean that fresh flowers last only a short time, so dried flowers have really come into their own. The choice is huge and the colour range exciting and there are dried decoration ideas to suit every taste and type of interior.

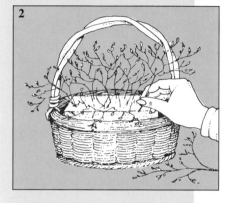

1 Wedge blocks of dry floral foam into base of the basket, making them level with the top edge.

2 Cover foam completely with a filler such as sea lavender.

3 Continue filling the basket, now using a mixture of other flowers and leaves. Aim to make a slightly domed outline.

▲ A large, rectangular basket made from sturdy twigs and with a stout handle makes a good container for a subtle mix of different dried flowers and leaves, including poppy seed heads, helichrysums, roses, sorrel, marigolds and amaranthus.

◀ This two-colour basket, with its elegant, twisted handle and lavender edging, contains another rich mixture of many different dried flowers. Helichrysums and deep red dahlias mix with love-in-a-mist and grey sea lavender. The effect relies on texture and colour, like the rug it sits on.

▶ Sparkling helichrysums fresh from harvesting are bright and shiny. The colours fade only very slowly if they are kept from strong sunlight. Used alone in a colourful mass, helichrysums are very effective.

1 *Put dry foam in the base of the basket.*

2 *Prepare flowers. Helichrysums will need to be wired. This is best done when they are fresh, but can be done once dry. Push a stub wire down through the centre of the bloom. Make a hook in the top end, which lodges into the flower head.*

3 *Fill whole basket with flowers, working across and making a neat, dense arrangement.*

119

1 *Begin by putting the bold-shaped foliage in place first.*

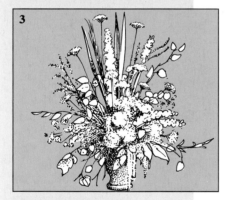

2 *Continue with the other foliage and material, filling in spaces and keeping an overall triangular outline in mind.*

3 *Finish off with the achillea and orange lanterns as the focal points.*

A collection of dried and preserved autumn flowers and foliage with a simple country feel. The beech leaves, molucella and fatsia leaves have been preserved in glycerine, which gives them a soft sheen. In contrast, the brilliant orange physalis lanterns and golden achillea glow warmly in a plain and simple setting.

The strong shapes of ornamental chillies are highlighted against a cottage window. The silvery seed covers of honesty come alive with the light shining through them and contrast with the heavy ears of wheat.

1 Put the fresh evergreen foliage in first, then add the honesty seed heads. You may need dry foam depending on your container.

2 Add the sprays of chilli peppers next, making the outline they create the furthest extent of the space they take up.

3 Finally add the stems of wheat and let them droop and curve downwards.

1 Pack dry foam into basket of your choice, keeping top of foam level with top of basket.

2 Make small bunches, if neccessary, of any small-scale flowers and tie with wire. Push into foam along with filler material. Work across basket.

3 Fill whole basket with bunches and single flowers until you have a dense, neat mass of flowers.

▲ *An unusual mixture of colours for a dried arragemment works very well here against the complementary backdrop of a deep blue and yellow rug. Dark blue larkspur and lavender are used with achillea, marigolds, poppy heads and soft green grasses.*

▶ *A gentle arrangement in peach and terracotta colours spills out from a shallow basket. Statice in several similar shades is put together with dried roses, santolina flowers and sprays of sea lavender.*

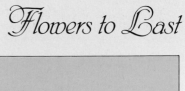

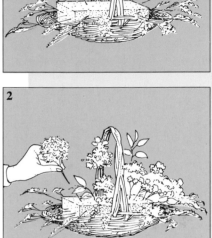

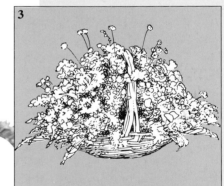

1 *Tape foam into shallow basket, slicing it lower if required.*

2 *Fill in outline with statice and leaves, making a spreading triangular shape.*

3 *Finish off with helichrysums and dried roses spread throughout the statice.*

BOOK TWO

Dried Flowers

BOOK TWO
Dried Flowers

Text by MING VEEVERS-CARTER

Photography by STEVE TANNER

Contents

Introduction and Commercial Drieds
pages 10-15

Home-preserved Drieds
pages 16-17

Equipment and Containers
pages 18-19

Techniques
pages 20-27

Decorative Gifts
pages 28-35

Weddings
pages 36-45

Valentines
pages 46-61

Spring
pages 62-73

Summer
pages 74-85

Autumn
pages 86-97

Winter
pages 98-109

Christmas
pages 110-123

Acknowledgements and Suppliers
page 124

Introduction

Dried flowers are no longer dull and lifeless winter substitutes for the abundance of fresh flowers available in the spring, summer and autumn. Improved techniques for drying have made commercially-dried flowers vibrant in colour, strong in shape and wide in variety. This high quality dried plant material lends itself to creating truly stunning and unique displays and decorations for the home for long-lasting pleasure, as exemplified by the designs in this book. However, many types of garden flower and foliage can be simply and successfully dried at home, which can be used in conjunction with exotic, commercially-dried items. Woods and waysides offer a rich harvest of cones and nuts, seedheads, pods and fungi for use in arrangements. Even artificial fruits and flowers can be imaginatively combined with natural dried material to produce richly-coloured displays.

Commercial Drieds
An increasingly wide range of commercially-dried plant material is available from a number of sources – florist and gift shops, department stores and garden centres. Dried flowers can also be mail-ordered together with all kinds of interesting dried items such as cones, lychin, moss, seedheads and pods, preserved leaves and fruits. Dried flowers are normally sold in bunches of one type, although occasionally mixed bunches are available, especially from gift shops. Cones, seedheads and pods can often be bought singly. Pot pourri mixtures, which are readily available, can be a good source of interesting and exotic cones and pods.

Before purchasing bunches of dried material, check the size and condition of each bunch. Select full-sized bunches that have not been flattened or squashed in any way. To test for damage, hold the bunch upside-down and shake gently (not vigorously!) to ensure that the flowers are not brittle and broken. Look for strength of colour in the flowers and check that it has not faded by comparing the colour of the outer flowers in the bunch with the ones in the centre.

Dyed Drieds
These are widely available in shops along with the natural-coloured material but I personally avoid using them since the colours tend to be overpowering and highly unnatural. Common dyed drieds include Gypsophila and a range of ornamental grasses such as quaking and pearl grass, rye and gypsy grass, as well as cereals such as oats and barley. Some of these items are also available in a bleached form.

Artificial Drieds
Poly-dried flowers have arrived relatively recently on the artificial flower market. They are made from polyester and heated to make the fabric shrivel slightly to give a dried flower appearance and texture. They have some advantages in that they are washable, highly durable and do not have to be wired as much as natural dried flowers for use in arrangements and decorations. However, they cannot quite emulate the effect of real dried flowers.

Paper and other kinds of artificial flowers can be used effectively in combination with natural dried items. Artificial fruits are also highly decorative. Do not be put off by their often crude-looking stems and leaves; judge the appearance of the fruit alone. Early in the new year is an ideal time to stock up on artificial items since many stores sell off excess Christmas stock cheaply.

Selection
The following pages present a selection of the most effective dried flowers, chosen for their shape, texture and colour, which can be purchased ready-dried or dried in the home (see pages 16-17).

Above: *Bunches of colourful* Helichrysum *being commercially air-dried.*

Rosa 'Minuet' Celosia Rosa 'Jaguar'

Rosa 'Mercedes' *Dark purple* Helichrysum *Salmon* Helichrysum

Yellow Achillea

Sunflower

Button chrysanthemum

Morrison

Carthamus

Rosa *'Golden Times'*

Rosa *'Vivaldi'* Peony Rosa *'Gerdo'*

Rosa *'Pink Delight'* Protea Rosa *'Kiss'*

Lilac Larkspur   *Baby* Eucalyptus   *Lilac* Achillea

Marjoram   Ageratum   *Lavender*

Home-preserved Drieds

Air-drying

This is the easiest and cheapest method of preserving plant material, although some plants are better preserved by using desiccants or glycerine (see below). Plants should be harvested on a dry day after any dew has evaporated. They should be grouped in small bunches, the stems bound together tightly near their bases with an elastic band (string can be used for woody stems since they are unlikely to shrink) and hung upside-down in a dry, dark and well-ventilated interior. A boiler or empty airing cupboard, a warm attic or over a radiator are all ideal sites. Leave the flowers to dry for several days – the exact length of time will vary according to atmospheric conditions and the type of plant. Check thoroughly to make sure that the flowers are completely dry before use.
Lavender must be harvested just before the buds begin to burst into flower. Dock flowers, cow parsley, roses and peonies should be cut when the blooms are at their peak. Make sure hydrangea heads are firm to the touch. These flowers, together with delphiniums, are best dried singly. Always dry more than you need since there will probably be some casualties.

Rose heads and other single flowerheads as well as tulip petals can be dried in a conventional oven on a very low heat. Keep checking the flowers to prevent them from browning.

Desiccants

These drying agents – sand, borax or silica gel – draw moisture from plants to preserve them. Silica gel, the most effective and the most expensive desiccant, is available usually in the form of white crystals from chemist shops or hardware stores. The stems of flowers to be dried in this way must be trimmed to 2.5 cm (1 in) in length. Insert a short stub wire inside each stalk while the flowers are fresh to minimise handling once they have been dried since they can be very brittle. A longer length of wire can then be bound onto the wire if necessary (see pages 24-25). Place a layer of crystals in the bottom of an airtight container and position flowers on the crystals (they should not be touching each other). Using a spoon, carefully cover the flowers with the crystals, inside and around each bloom, taking care not to distort their shape. When fully covered, replace the lid of the container and store in a warm place for about 48 hours. Unearth the flowers with great care to avoid damage.

For quick results, put the crystals in a shallow microwave-proof dish, add flowerheads and place in a microwave oven. 'Cook' on the highest setting for 5 to 7 minutes, checking every 30 seconds when almost ready. Leave the flowers to cool in the crystals for about 10-15 minutes before removing.

Borax is a cheaper desiccant but takes longer to work – about 10 days. Mix with dry silver sand, three parts borax to two parts sand, and use in the same way as the silica gel.

Use desiccants to preserve roses, peonies, lilies, freesias, fuschias and anemones.

Glycerining

This method is best used to preserve deciduous and evergreen foliage. Make a mixture of one part glycerine to two parts boiling water and pour into a fairly tall, narrow container. Stand stems in about 8-10 cm (3-4 in) of the mixture. Hammer the ends of woody stems to facilitate absorption. Leave for a week and check leaves for pliability. Some stems may require longer treatment. Individual leaves can be glycerined by immersing entirely in the mixture in a shallow container. Some flowerheads can be effectively preserved in this way, such as roses and anemones.

Right: *A bunch of roses in their fresh state and after being air-dried. The blooms shrink a good deal but also open out a little after they have been hanging up. The colours have been well preserved although they do change in hue.*

17

Equipment

Dry florist's foam is generally essential in making an arrangement. There are blocks that can be easily cut and shaped to fit containers, as a base in which to position stems (see opposite); balls of varying sizes which can be used for topiaries (page 26), rose or bay balls (pages 58 and 23); cones which can also be used for topiaries (page 114) and rings used as a base for wreaths (pages 68-69). Nylon-reinforced plaster is ideal for setting trunks in pots when making topiaries (page 26). A glue gun is an excellent tool and can be used to glue all kinds of items onto wreaths, baskets, wood and fabric. The glue is hot so extra care must be taken to avoid burning the fingers. There are various different types and thicknesses of wire (page 25), but I only use four kinds: narrow and thick silver wire for fine work, for example headdresses (the thicker is best); 22 gauge stem wires, which are long and narrow, used for wiring light bunches or single stems; and 18 gauge stem wires, which are thicker versions of the 22 gauge and used for heavier items. Stem binding tape has two purposes (page 25): it gives an extra hold to wire stems and conceals the wire or green sticks (see below). Anchor tape is a strong adhesive tape used to secure foam and moss to containers (see opposite). Green canes are used for making stems longer. Candle holders are useful for holding candles firmly in place. They also make the replacement of candles easy to achieve. Wire-edged ribbon is considerably more expensive than ordinary ribbon but can be moulded into a variety of shapes that will hold.

Containers

Choosing your container is as important as selecting your flowers. Its size, shape and texture is important and will dictate to a certain extent the shape of the arrangement. As an approximate guide, the arrangement should be the twice the height again as the pot and twice the width.

into the sides of the foam to soften the rim of the container. For narrow-necked containers, cut the foam a fraction bigger than the neck width and push into the pot. The foam should also have two-thirds of its length inside the container. When arranging, push wire stems all the way down through the foam and do not remove and insert stems too often, since the foam will disintegrate. Glass containers must first be filled, for example with pot pourri, moss, pebbles, nuts, shells, beans, pasta, fabric or paper, to conceal the foam. If using paper or fabric, line container first, then add a piece of foam 2.5 cm (1 in) smaller than the pot. Otherwise, place the foam in the container and fill around the edge. Cover with moss and tape in place. For a basket, fill with a piece of foam slightly bigger than the container. Trim the corners and cover with moss. Cut a piece of wire netting about 2.5 cm (1 in) smaller than the basket. Position on top of moss and attach to basket by threading black reel wire through the basket rim and netting, and twisting wire ends together. Repeat at intervals around the basket rim.

Covering a footed bowl

Spread out a piece of fabric right side down and place the pot in the centre. From underneath, gather up the fabric around the bowl's 'neck' and hold in place with one hand. Turn the bowl upside down and secure fabric to neck with a 22 gauge wire. Holding pot around neck, pull fabric downwards

gently to make even gathers all the way round. Now turn upright again and tuck excess fabric into the top of the pot.

Pinning moss to foam

Make pins from 18 or 22 gauge stem wire by cutting into 7.5-10 cm (3-4 in) lengths and bending in half. Use to pin plastic backing to moss (page 20) and moss or strings of chillies to foam.

Dry foam fillings

Shallow bowls, flat dishes or plastic trays are tightly filled with foam to a higher level than the pot rim. Cover with a little sphagnum moss and secure in place with adhesive tape. A piece of foam can be glued inside a footed bowl with strong adhesive when tape or wire (see below) would show, but the container could not then be used for another purpose. Trim the corners of the foam to fit and make sure it sits at least 2.5 cm (1 in) above the pot rim. This enables stems to be inserted diagonally

Techniques

Ribbon bows

Single bow with tails: *Make a loop in the ribbon on either side of your thumb and forefinger leaving a similar length of hanging ribbon on either side as tails. Cut ribbon and twist one end of a 22 gauge stem wire around the middle.*

Double-looped bow: *As above except make 2 loops either side instead of one. To finish bow, cut a small length of ribbon and tie around the middle to cover the wire. Trim off excess ribbon at the bow back.*

Single loop without tails: *As single bow but do not make tails. Tuck the short ribbon ends into the loops and wire as before.*

Fabric bows

Cut a strip of fabric four times the required width and fold in half lengthways. Fold in half again, bringing the raw long edges to meet the fold, and glue. Cut the short ends diagonally, turn under the raw edges and glue. Make a bow with or without tails. To make the 'knot', cut a narrow length of fabric and with the reverse facing, fold the raw long edges into the middle, overlap and glue. Tie around the middle of the bow and cut off excess, or use this to form tails. Use the glue sparingly so that it does not seep through the fabric.

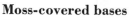

Moss-covered bases

Moss rope: *Cut a strip of wire netting 20 cm (8 in) wide. Fill with sphagnum moss, packing tightly since the tube needs to be quite solid. Wrap the netting around the moss and twist the cut wire ends around the netting to secure.*

Dry foam block: *Cut a piece of wire netting roughly twice the size of the block(s). Line the netting with a thin layer of moss and wrap around the block. Along the length of the block, twist the cut wire ends around the netting to secure. Cut away the excess netting at the sides of the block and twist the cut ends onto the netting as before.*

Backing dry foam block: *Place moss and wire covered block face down. Cut a piece of double thickness black plastic a little larger than the block. Place over the base of the block and pin to the sides with wire pins made from 18 gauge wires cut into short lengths and bent in half. The plastic should not overlap the base onto the sides by more than 1.2 cm (½ in). The backing protects any surface upon which the block may be placed.*

Cutting stems

To cut Eucalyptus, hold the leaves back and cut as close as possible to the next set of leaves. Repeat all the way down the stem until the latter begins to thicken. This procedure allows the maxiumum use of the stem. With multi-branched stems, cut undivided heads for use as they are, or small sprigs with 5-cm (2-in) stems to be wired for use in headdresses and small garlands. Stems 12.5-15 cm (5-6 in) in length are suitable for standard arrangements.

Bay leaf ball

Select several medium-sized fresh bay leaves and a medium-sized dry foam ball. Glue leaves to the ball using transparent-drying adhesive, beginning in the middle, generously overlapping the leaves. Slot other leaves behind and cover the ball completely. The leaves will shrink when they dry, so it is important to overlap them sufficiently.

Wiring a terracotta pot

Place a small piece of dry foam into a pot so that it fits snugly. Thread an 18 gauge wire through the bottom of the pot and between the foam and the side of the pot. The pot can then be wired onto a basket, moss rope or wreath.

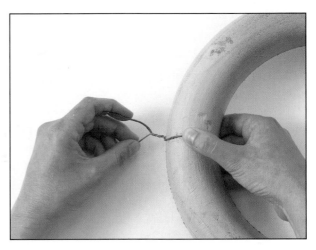

Wiring a wreath

Cover an 18 gauge wire with stem binding tape and wrap around a wreath once only. Twist the ends of the wire tightly, so that the wire cannot move around the ring. Leave the ends of the wire apart so that they can be twisted onto a hook, around a curtain rail or whatever the wreath will be hung from. If the wreath is very thick and one wire is not long enough, twist two wires together and cover with stem binding tape.

Mounting candles

If using chunky beeswax candles, simply insert 2 or three pieces of cane into the bottom of the candle by not more than 2.5 cm (1 in). Attach legs to other thick candles by cutting 10-cm (4-in) pieces of cane. Hold one piece against the side of the candle and bind onto the candle with green adhesive tape. Then add the next 'leg' and bind as before. When all legs are in place, bind all together a few more times to secure. Legs can be attached to narrow candles, but candle holders are more practical.

Wiring stems

When decorating with or arranging dried flowers, it is best to attach the flowers, seedheads etc - either singly or in bunches - to lengths of wire, since their own stems are often too thick or brittle. Wiring also helps to create a more solid arrangement, as opposed to an airy, wispy effect. You will need 18 or 22 gauge stem wires, the 18 gauge being the strongest and used if the wire is to be the only support for the bunch. The 22 gauge wire is suitable for mounting bunches onto canes, used to create tall stems.

Take a bunch of dried material and cut stems to the required length - usually 12.5-17.5 cm (5-7 in). Hold stems together tightly at the bottom between thumb and forefinger. Bend a wire about two-thirds of the way along its length to from a loop. Place the loop under the bunch and hold in place with the third finger. Firmly twist the longer portion of the wire 5 or 6 times around the bunch, but not too tightly as to break the stems. To mount onto a cane, repeat the process but hold the cane under the bunch as you wire. Cinnamon sticks are available in a variety of sizes. Roll a bunch together in the hand to make them fit together. Hold the bunch tightly, place a wire around the middle and twist the ends together several times. The wire should be tight enough to cut into the bark slightly.

Nuts, pomegranates, cones, artichokes and single flowerheads

To wire a walnut, dip the end of a 22 gauge wire into latex-based adhesive, then push into the nut base where the two halves join. Leave to dry. Pomegranates are available loose, which can be glued onto 18 gauge wires, or ready glued to stems. They can also be wired onto canes. Small and medium-sized cones are wired with 22 gauge wires; larger cones require 18 gauge wires. Very large cones can be wired onto bamboo canes with 18 gauge wire. Loop a wire around the cone close to the base. Twist the ends together tightly. Trim the stems of artichokes to 2.5 cm (1 in) in length. Wind the wire through the leaves at the base, as for the cone, and twist the ends around the stem. Single flowers, such as roses, are wired in the same way as bunches.

Headdresses and small garlands

Use silver wires since they are fine but firm enough to take the weight of small flowers. Silver wire comes in 2 thicknesses – the thicker is best. Cut flowers from stems, either singly or in bunches. Hold firmly between thumb and forefinger. Make a loop in a length of wire and hold under the short stem. Wind one end around the length of stem about 6 times keeping the wire taut.

Binding stems

Tightly wind stem binding tape twice around the top of a wired stem or bunch to cover the wire. Hold firmly between thumb and forefinger and with the other hand, pull the tape downwards so that it stretches. Turn the stem between thumb and fore-finger while continuing to pull the tape downwards so that it twists around the length of wire. Body heat causes tape to stick to itself. Keep stretching for good adhesion and a thin covering.

Circlet

Overlap two 18 gauge wires by at least 10 cm (4 in). Twist a silver wire around the thicker wire, beginning at the top. Bind the entire length of wire with stem binding tape. Bend one end of the wire into a loop and bind in place with the tape. Bend the other end into a hook.

Bridesmaid's posy handle

Leaving a free length of ribbon 25 cm (10 in) in length, hold ribbon to the top of the handle and run the remainder of the ribbon downwards over the bottom of the handle, then upwards to the top of the handle. Hold both parts of the ribbon together with one hand. With the other hand, wrap the uncut ribbon down the handle. At this stage, the ribbon should be wrong side facing. At the bottom of the handle, fold over the excess ribbon and wrap with the ribbon, which should be twisted so that the right side is now facing. Work upwards to the handle top and tie the ribbon onto the free length. Make a simple bow and tie to the top of the handle with a double knot. Insert a long pearl-ended pin into the centre of the bow and push up through the posy.

Using bung moss

Use a pair of florist's scissors to trim away the root portion of the bung moss before use. This enables the moss to fit smoothly onto a surface as well as making it easier to glue.

To make a topiary

1 Fill a pot three-quarters full with nylon-reinforced plaster or quick-drying plaster. The former is cleaner and heavier. If using the latter, first place some stones in the bottom of the pot. This kind of plaster will harden in a few minutes, while the reinforced type will take up to 24 hours to dry. Set the main trunk in the centre of the pot, then branches around the trunk, if desired. Wire the branches to the trunk at the bottom and top. Cut a hole the same circumference as the trunk and approximately 5 cm (2 in) deep in a dry foam ball. Cut a piece of wire netting large enough to cover the ball. Wrap around the ball keeping the hole clear of wire.

2 Squeeze some glue from a glue gun into the hole and push the ball onto the trunk. Leave to dry. Thread a 22 gauge wire through the netting at the ball base and around the trunk. Twist the ends tightly to secure. Repeat at equal intervals around the trunk.

3 Push wired items or stems into the ball beginning at the middle top. Work around and down, keeping the dried materials very close together.

4 To create a different-shaped topiary, select dry foam blocks to give the required size. Glue blocks together using a glue gun. When dry, cut the foam to a desired shape. A slightly oval shape is effective for a moss topiary. Treat in the same way as the foam ball.

Decorative Gifts

Surprise and delight your family and friends by making stylish and individual dried flower gifts especially for them. Here is a range of inspirational ideas, from exquisitely-packaged pot pourri to a rustic wreath of culinary herbs, both practical and decorative. Alternatively, enhance any gift package with an elegant dried flower decoration.

Decorative Gifts

◀ Decorate a brightly-coloured box with matching ribbon and fill with a fragrant and eye-catching pot pourri mixture – perhaps consisting of flowers and herbs gathered from your garden throughout the spring and summer. We chose yellow ('Golden Times'), red ('Jaguar') and orange ('Tennessee') roses; daffodil heads and pumpkin seeds. Place your ingredients in a bowl and mix to evenly disperse. Add a few drops of rose essential oil or another oil of your choice drop by drop. Transfer mixture to a plastic bag and seal. Leave in a dark, cool place for about 6 weeks. Shake the bag thoroughly twice a week.

▶ Gift packages for any occasion can be transformed from the commonplace with the simple addition of dried flowerheads and other material. Keep the glue gun away from the parcel when gluing the flowers and be careful not to burn your fingers when applying hot glue to small dried items. You can use a strong, tube adhesive instead, but avoid any direct contact with the fingers.

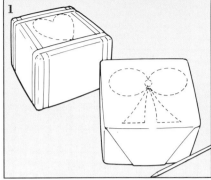

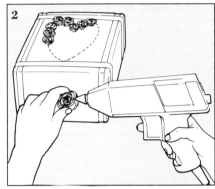

1 *Wrap parcels and decorate with ribbon. Draw outlines of the designs in pencil onto the parcels.*

2 *Using a glue gun, apply glue to the bottom of each flower and position.*

3 *Glue on nuts and fruits one at a time.*

◄ Napkins can be effectively decorated for a celebration table using wire-edged ribbon, which can be arranged to create attractive shapes, flowerheads, cones or seedheads. Choose colours and textures to ccordinate with the overall colour scheme or theme of the table.

► A dainty and delightful basket arrangement that would make an elegant addition to a treasured friend or relative's beside or dressing table.

You will need:
2 bunches lavender
1 bunch red roses
1 bunch marjoram
1 bunch Eucalyptus
1 bunch orange Helichrysum
7 open orange roses
Wire roses, Helichrysum and Eucalyptus in groups of three stems, but marjoram and lavender in small bunches. Use 22 gauge wire and bind with tape (pages 24-25).

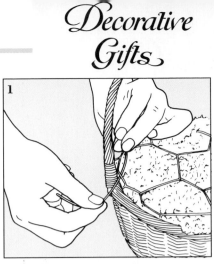

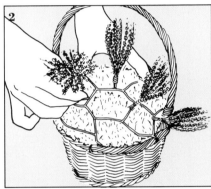

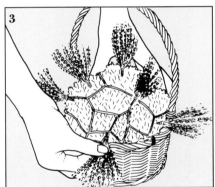

1 *Cut block of oasis to fit snugly in basket. Cover lightly with moss and wire netting.*

2 *Position bunches of either lavender or marjoram to create the basic shape.*

3 *At the front of the basket, gently bend the bunches downwards to cover the edge.*

◄ *Turn an ordinary wicker basket into an original and highly attractive gift by decorating the outside with a colourful variety of dried and artificial items. For this design, we used tree mushrooms, white paper flowers, tree lychin moss, small poppy seedheads, florets of artificial hydrangea and petals of a 'Minuet' rose. Simply apply glue from a glue gun to the bottom of each item and position on the basket.*

► *This inviting herbal wreath makes the ideal gift for any cook. It will bring natural fragrance to the kitchen as well as a ready supply of herbs for culinary purposes.*

You will need:
A twig ring
1 bunch fresh rosemary
1 bunch marjoram
5 bushy stems fresh bay
70 dried chillies
Trim stems of marjoram and rosemary to 17.5 cm (7 in) in length; bay leaves can be shorter.

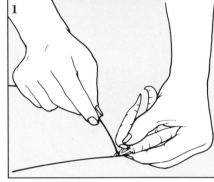

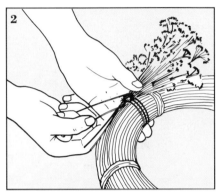

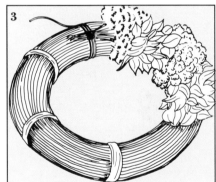

1 *Attach a wire to hang the wreath (page 23). Using silver reel wire, wire together bunches of chillies, then wire with 22 gauge stem wires and bind with stem binding tape (pages 24-25).*

2 *Wire a bunch of marjoram to ring.*

3 *Add chillies, bay then rosemary. Repeat pattern until wreath is complete.*

Weddings

Dried flowers offer a highly practical and versatile alternative to fresh flowers for weddings. Obviously their use avoids altogether the major problem of wilting on a hot day. Vibrantly-coloured dried material can be combined to create dramatic headdresses, corsages and posies, which can all be made well in advance of the big day.

◀ This charming little basket is ideal for a young bridesmaid to hold at a country wedding in place of a posy. The flowers are simply glued to the rim of the basket. It can be filled with small flowerheads and leaves, to be showered over the happy couple!

You will need:
1 bunch Helichrysum
½ bunch Carthamus
½ bunch cluster-flowered Helichrysum
6 proteas
  5 open roses ('Golden Times')
  1 stem bright blue Delphinium

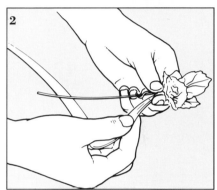

To make a bridesmaid's pomander, wrap a dry foam ball in a square of fabric, gather at the top and secure with a 22 gauge wire. Trim excess fabric to 10 cm (4 in) above wire. Fold over and tuck in rough fabric edges. Make a fabric ribbon and tie on. Glue flowerheads around the wire.

1 For the corsage, cover a 10-cm (4-in) piece of 18 gauge wire with stem binding tape (page 25). Wire and bind flowerheads and leaves (pages 24-25). Twist a wired leaf onto one end of a length of wire and bind with stem binding tape. Add a wired flower below and twist onto leaf wire.

2 Cover wire with stem binding tape. Continue adding flowers and bind with tape. Trim excess wires as you work.

▶ *To make a more secure decoration for the pomander, wire flowers onto a wire ring following the instructions for the champagne bottle wreath on page 49, then attach to the pomander around the 'neck'. These dainty decorations are light and easy for junior bridesmaids to hold.*

39

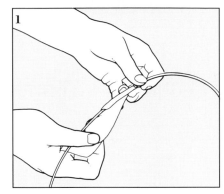

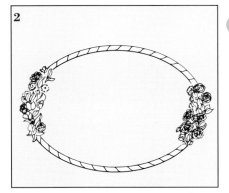

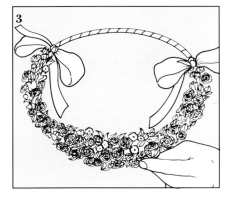

1 *Bind hoop tightly with ribbon.*

2 *Cut flowers from stems at the top and spread on a tray. Measure 10 cm (4 in) either side of the top middle point of hoop. Begin gluing small flowerheads to hoop.*

3 *Use larger flowers at the centre bottom for balance. Make two small bows (pages 20-21) and attach to hoop.*

▲ *This elegant hoop makes an unusual alternative to the more traditional posy. The bows can be omitted for a simpler, cleaner effect.*

▶ *Give your wedding gifts a chic personal touch by gluing dried flowers – either single heads or bunches – onto giftwrap or decorative ribbon. Here, we have used 2 peony heads and a small bunch of lavender with pale blue wire-edged ribbon for the white package; a glycerined mauve anemone (page 16) with gold ribbon for the blue/gold marbled box.*

◄ *The frosted blue hydrangea and touches of cow parsley give a lacy quality to these decorative accessories. Follow the instructions on page 33 to make the basket, using the bunches of red roses to create the basic shape. To make the headdress, refer to the instructions on page 45.*

For both the basket and the headdress, you will need:
1 bunch cow parsley
40 stems dark red roses ('Jaguar')
10 stems miniature pink species roses ('Pink Delight')
10 peonies
2 heads hydrangea

For the bouquet, you will need:
30-40 stems poly-dried flowers
3 m (3⅓ yd) x 3-cm (1¼-in) wide ribbon
Wire flowerheads with 22 gauge wires (pages 24-25) – their original stems are far too heavy. Cover wire with stem binding tape (page 25) and group in jars or vases to make selection easier.

◄ *Poly-dried flowers are an effective artificial alternative to real dried flowers. Made from polyester, they are able to withstand considerable wear and tear. Make a headdress from poly-dried flowers to match the bouquet following the instructions on page 45.*

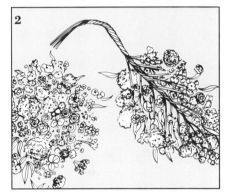

1 *Begin with the bottom of the bouquet. Twist wired stems of flowers and leaves onto each other to form a soft, oval-shaped 'tail'. Continue to add stems until the tail is at least 25 cm (10 in) long. Bend the wire ends downwards to form a handle at least 15 cm (6 in) away from the flowers.*

2 *Make a light posy 20-25 cm (8-10 in) in diameter with silver reel wire, bind stem of posy to stem of 'tail' below handle. Hold the bouquet's handle in front of a mirror and add more flowers to fill any gaps. Trim excess wires and cut handle to hand size. Cover well with stem binding tape. Cover with ribbon and add bow (pages 26-27).*

You will need:
2 bunches marjoram
2 bunches lavender
27 orange roses, one large
20 red roses
Wire roses singly; marjoram and lavender in small bunches (pages 24-25) using 22 gauge wires. Cover wire with stem binding tape (page 25).

1 Begin with the large rose in the centre and surround with marjoram. Bind the stems together with silver reel wire where your hand is holding the bouquet. Add next set of flowers – about 5 stems – and wire. Turn the posy as you work.

2 Check side of posy occasionally to make sure that you are creating a domed shape. When complete, trim wire stems and bind with stem binding tape (page 25). Cover handle with ribbon (pages 26-27).

▶ *When making the posy, once you have covered stems with stem binding tape, place flowers in jars — the same type in one jar — for easy access and selection.*

For the headdress you will need:
6-8 thimble-sized terracotta pots
Tiny bunches of various dried
* flowers*
Single flowerheads, eg roses,
* sunflowers and marigolds*
15 x 7.5-cm (3-in) squares fabric
Wire tiny bunches and single flowerheads onto silver wires and cover with stem binding tape (page 25). Wire terracotta pots (page 23) and fill each with a wired flowerhead, the wire end fed through the hole in the pot bottom. Gather up corners of each fabric square and wire with silver wire. Bind with stem binding tape.

◀ *You will need to build up your confidence and competence before attempting this formal, Victorian-style posy, but your endeavours will be well rewarded.*

1 *Make a circlet (page 25). Begin at hook end and twist wired flowers etc onto circlet (page 49). Trim excess wires as you work. Finish 7.5 cm (3 in) from loop. Make a corsage (page 39) using same flowers as in first 10 cm (4 in) of circlet. Using a silver wire covered with stem binding tape (page 25), attach corsage in three places to circlet, the wire end of corsage tucking under flowers on circlet.*

2 *For posy, wire flowers with 22 gauge wires and cover with stem binding tape (pages 24-25). Take 5-8 stems and tightly bind together 12.5 cm (5 in) from the flowerheads (5-7.5 cm/2-3 in for small bridesmaids) using silver reel wire. Whilst turning stems in one hand, open them out to create a frame. Add other flowers, binding one stem in place at a time. Finally, trim wires, bind handle with tape and ribbon (pages 26-27).*

Valentines

Flowers are universally chosen to mark the great romantic milestones - courtship; engagement; wedding and anniversary. The versatility of dried flowers offers the opportunity to create a wide variety of displays and decorations of lasting significance.

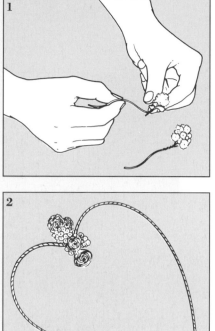

You will need:
2 bunches Ageratum
100 stems red roses
Wire rose heads singly with silver
wires and cover with stem binding
tape (page 25). Wire Ageratum
into groups of 5 heads and bind.

1 *Use silver wire to join two 18*
gauge wires together and bind
with stem binding tape (page 25).
Bend wire to form shape. Attach
ends together by forming a loop
and hook (page 25).

2 *Twist flowers onto heart starting*
from the middle top and working
outwards and downwards. Keep
the flowers even all the way
around.

◀ *A stunning heart-shaped wreath to adorn a wall or door at a wedding or anniversary reception. When wiring the flowers to the wreath, rest the heart on a work surface.*

▶ *A delightful decoration for a celebratory bottle of bubbly. It is important to select vividly-coloured flowers to contrast with the colour of the bottle. Lay flowers out on your work surface to see how they work together before wiring.*

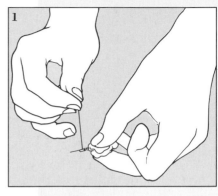

1 *Select a few small brightly-coloured flowers and bind with silver wires (page 25). Bind with stem binding tape (page 25).*

2 *Bend an 18 gauge wire into a hoop, overlap ends and twist together. Cover with stem binding tape. Bind flowers onto hoop one at a time, making 3 or 4 twists then trimming excess wire. Continue until hoop is full. To add last flower, pull other flowers away slightly, wire on flower and re-arrange others.*

◀ *A rich arrangement to crown an intimate dining table or grace a dressing table. Refer to the instructions on page 103 to create the arrangement, using the bunches of marjoram to set the basic shape. But first position the beeswax candle in the centre of the foam by inserting short lengths of green cane into the bottom of the candle (page 23).*

You will need:
2 bunches marjoram
1 bunch globe amaranth
1 bunch green golden rod
20 red roses
15 open peach roses
A chunky beeswax candle

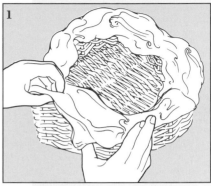

Line the basket with plastic, then cover with fabric. The plastic will prevent any essential oils from seeping through the basket onto the table.

1 *Glue ribbon onto basket. Squeeze a small amount of glue from a glue gun, wait a few seconds then press ribbon onto glue, thus avoiding any risk of burning your fingers.*

2 *Cut roses from stems entirely. Squeeze a little glue onto underside of each rose and hold in place on the basket until glue dries. When finished, remove any strands of glue. Fill basket with hydrangea florets and add a few drops of essential oil if desired.*

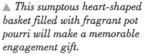

▲ *This sumptous heart-shaped basket filled with fragrant pot pourri will make a memorable engagement gift.*

You will need:
30-35 roses
2 heads hydrangea
2 m (2¼ yd) wire-edged ribbon

◀ *There are many different styles of basket available and they can all be decorated to great effect with dried flowers. You will enjoy looking out for new varieties to transform into eye-catching decorations for the home. Our wicker basket has holders for candles and has been decorated with assorted pink roses interspersed with a few rose leaves.*

▶ *This is a facing arrangement, ie it is designed to be viewed from the front or sides; it is not an all-round arrangement. This is an extravagant display for a very special occasion, to stand in an empty fireplace or against a wall.*

You will need:
5 bunches cones
4 bunches peach roses
3-5 bunches marjoram
3 bunches assorted roses
2 bunches mixed species roses
2 bunches green golden rod
15 cinnamon sticks
7 heads hydrangea
5 stems artificial fruits
1 m (1⅛ yd) silk

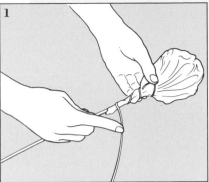

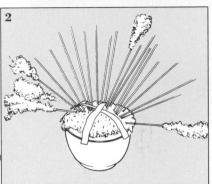

Fill pot with dry foam, making sure it fits securely. Cover lightly with moss and tape in place.

1 Cut the silk into nine squares. Gather up corners, hold tightly together and bind with silver wire. Wire each gathered fabric piece onto a green cane using 22 gauge wire (pages 24-25). Tuck in any rough edges. Bind with stem binding tape. Wire bunches of flowers, fruits, cones and cinnamon sticks onto canes and bind (pages 24-25).

2 Begin at back of pot and place first bunch of flowers three-quarters of the way back from front of pot. Place bunches around outer edge and middle of arrangement to make a basic frame in which to work. Fill in with other canes pushing some deeper into the foam to give dimension.

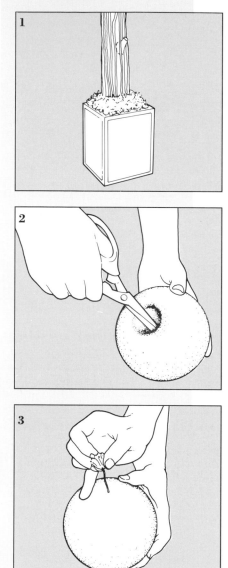

1 *Push pole into plaster. Trim leaves from rose stems and place around pole. Push stems into plaster and wire to pole at top.*

2 *Cut a small hole in foam ball (page 26), fill with glue and push onto pole. Leave to set.*

3 *Push roses into ball starting at the top. Tie ribbon around poles and cover plaster with moss.*

◄ *This pair of elegant rose topiaries would make an unusual mantelpiece display for a social gathering to celebrate a special anniversary.*

You will need:
2 birch poles 2.5-3.75cm (1-1½ in) in diameter, 30cm (12 in) in length
200 roses
A little moss
1 m (1⅛ yd) ribbon
Line two pots with plastic and fill a half to three-quarters full with nylon-reinforced plaster (page 26). Cut roses from stems leaving 2.5 cm (1 in) of stem on flowers. Do not discard stems.

▶ *In this opulent arrangement, bunches of crimson, deep pink, pale pink and pale yellow roses are packed closely together to form a solid domed shape, broken at intervals with contrasting sprigs of blue/green Eucalyptus (pages 22-23).*

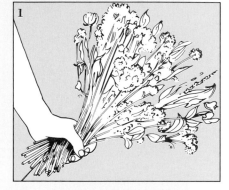

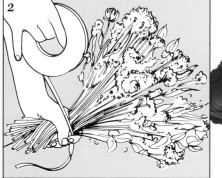

You will need:
2 bunches marjoram
40 roses
1 m (1⅛ yd) ribbon
Roses must be stripped of leaves
and thorns to about three-quarters
of the way up stems.

1 *Separate stems of dried material*
so they can be picked up easily with
one hand. Hold a small bunch of
stems in one hand, then add one
stem at a time, spiralling the stems
as you go. Flowers should get
shorter around outer edge.

2 *Bind stems together with wire*
or stem binding tape. Cover with
ribbon and a bow (pages 20-21).
Trim stems so posy can stand.

◀ *A posy with a difference - the stems are twisted so that they splay, enabling it to stand upright. A dramatic centrepiece for a large-scale celebration dining or buffet table.*

▶ *These are romantic gifts or decorations with a distinctively Victorian feel. Follow the instructions on page 58 to make the pomander. Make a bow (pages 20-21) and push wire stems into the bottom of the ball. Wire a loop of fabric and insert into the ball top to hang. A plain wooden picture frame can be enhanced by gluing on lychin moss and rose heads.*

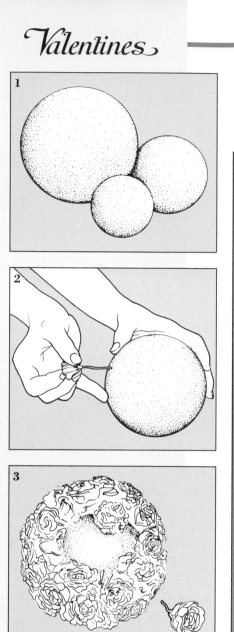

1 Select size of foam ball required. Trim rose stems to 2.5 cm (1 in) in length.

2 Hold ball in palm of the hand. Push roses into foam close together.

3 Complete one side of ball, turn over and gently continue inserting roses into ball until covered entirely.

◀ *Even the smallest size of foam ball requires a great many roses to fully cover it. However, if you wanted to group a few rose balls in a bowl, you could leave the foam bare where it was not visible, to use fewer roses. Drape ribbon or fabric around the balls to conceal any bare patches.*

You will need:
7.5-12.5 cm (3-5 in) dry foam balls
100 roses (for 10 cm/4 in balls)

▲ *Delight a loved one or a bride to be with a collection of pretty and fragrant homemade pomanders. Cut a square or circular piece of muslin and fill with lavender or a pot pourri (page 30). Gather the edges of the muslin together and tie with narrow string. Trim excess muslin if necessary. Place the bag upright in the centre of a piece of fabric. Gather up the edges around the bag and fasten at the 'neck' with silver reel wire. Cover with coordinating ribbon and tie the end in a loop. Tuck the raw edges of the fabric down into the neck of the bag, arranging the fabric into attractive folds.*

◄ These miniature terracotta pot arrangements would make unusual table decorations for a celebration of romance. Fill the pots tightly with foam and insert trimmed rose stems, small bunches of marjoram or lavender. Push a short length of green cane into the bottom of the candle (page 23) and insert into the foam.

▶ A subtle but beautiful miniature arrangement. Bend the bunches at the front forwards over the edge of the pot to create a softer effect. When arranging, stand back from the arrangement at intervals to check the overall shape.

You will need:
2 bunches blue larkspur
1 bunch chamomile daisy
20 assorted roses
5 pink peonies
5 dark purple peonies
1 stem artificial fruits

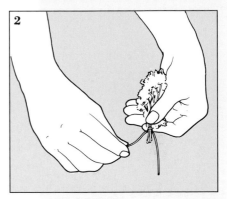

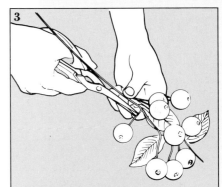

1 Push a slightly over-sized block of foam into pot. Trim corners, cover lightly with moss and tape in place.

2 Wire flowers in small bunches with 22 gauge wires (pages 24-25) to make 7.5 cm (3 in) stems and bind with stem binding tape (page 25). There is no need to wire peonies.

3 Cut fruit from stem, wire and bind as above. Start with peonies then add other flowers.

Spring

Herald the awakening of spring by creating a unique decoration or display for the home that exploits woodland textures and natural colours bringing with it a feeling of re-birth and rejuvenation. Here we present novel ideas for gifts, arrangements for Eastertide as well as table centrepieces.

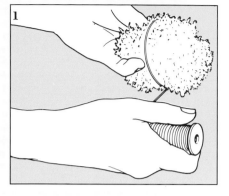

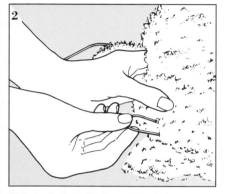

Lay a thick layer of moss over the tray or board and bind in place with black reel wire. Complete one side, then turn over and cover the other side.

1 To make bunny, tightly bind a handful of moss. Add more moss and bind until the body is complete. Make ears and tail in the same way and bind onto body. Use the berries for eyes and nose.

2 Cut several 18 gauge wires into three pieces and bend each into a hairpin shape. Use to pin bunny to tray or board.

◀ *A country bunny decoration makes an appropriate centrepiece for Easter. If you intend to move him around, glue the bung and lychin moss to the sphagnum moss.*

You will need:
A rectangular piece of wood or
*   standard-sized tray*
Sphagnum moss, fresh
Bung and lychin moss
Artificial mushrooms
1 stem artificial berries

▲ *Present a gift of fresh, potted herbs or other plants in a woodland-inspired box. Select a sturdy fruit or moss box and bind sphagnum moss to the sides with black reel wire. Line box with thick plastic or a plant tray.*

Thread twigs through the wire on the box sides. and insert flower stems into the moss to add colour.

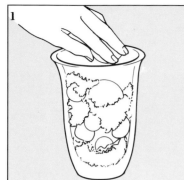

You will need:
2 bunches globe amaranth
18 stems Anaphalis (pearl
  everlasting)
15 stems cones
10 cinnamon sticks
9 proteas
6 artichoke heads
  3 large sea sponges
  Ground lychin and bung moss
Pebbles

◀ The lychin moss should be
soaked in warm water and
squeezed as dry as possible before
being used in the arrangement.
It will dry in place, so
there is no need to wire.

▶ Stripped branches of contorted
willow can be presented in an
interesting container to create a
minimalistic yet atmospheric
display. The shape of the
arrangement can be changed from
time to time for added interest —
from windswept to a wide and
shallow dome or triangle.

1 *Place bung moss into a vase
then some pebbles to fill one-third.
Add a block of dry foam. Add
more moss and pebbles.*

2 *Wire cinnamon sticks and other
drieds (pages 24-25). Bind with
stem binding tape (page 25).
Make holes in sea sponges for
wiring.*

3 *Push wire through the holes and
twist. Position sea sponge, then
other material. Add soaked and
squeezed moss.*

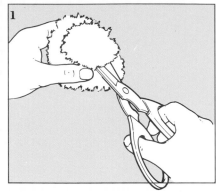

1

2

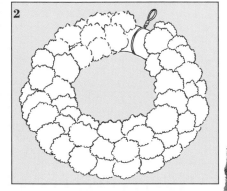

3

1 *Attach wire to ring for hanging (page 23). Place ring on a well-protected surface. Trim root base from moss (page 26).*

2 *Squeeze a small amount of glue onto underside of moss. Position clumps close together on ring – hold in position until set.*

3 *Leave 2.5 cm (1 in) of bare ring for a ribbon bow (pages 20-21). Glue on button chrysanthemums in between moss clumps.*

You will need:
A dry foam ring
Bung moss
Button chrysanthemums

▲ *An attractive ring that brings the suggestion of fresh spring grass into the home.*

1 Cover underside of ring in fabric. Glue to sides of ring to a level of 1 cm (½ in).

2 Apply glue to the reverse of the fabric and press in place. Be very careful not to burn your fingers.

3 Wire flowers and cover with stem binding tape (pages 24-25). Trim wires so that they do not pierce underside of wreath when mounted.

You will need:
A foam ring 30 cm (12 in) in diameter
3 bunches grasses
1 bunch blue larkspur
1 bunch Alchemilla
20 stems roses
20 tree mushrooms
6 artificial mushrooms
3 heads hydrangea

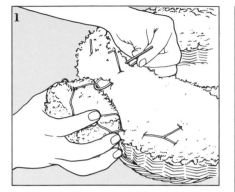

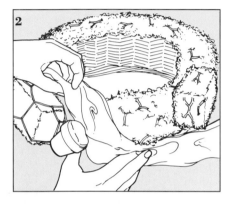

Wire roses, larkspur and Alchemilla in small bunches; wire cinnamon sticks in pairs and pomegranates (pages 24-25). Trim stems of peonies — there is no need to wire.

1 *Make a 7.5-cm (3-in) moss rope (page 21). Wire to rim of basket. Cut a foam block into eighths. Cover pieces in moss and wire netting (page 21). Wire at intervals to rope. Fill pots with foam and wire up (page 23). Attach to moss rope close to blocks.*

2 *Drape fabric between blocks and secure in place with 22 gauge wires. Fill blocks and pots with dried material. Tie decorative paper rope at intervals around the fabric swags.*

▲ *You will need:*
6 mini terracotta pots
2 bunches Alchemilla
1 bunch blue larkspur
40 yellow roses
12 dark purple peonies
10 pomegranates
Large bag cinnamon sticks
Sphagnum moss
1 m (1⅛ yd) narrow rope
1 m (1⅛ yd) blue silk

▶ *You will need:*
3 bunches glycerined Eucalyptus
3 bunches cat mint
80 peach roses
15 pomegranates
Sphagnum moss
3 candles
2 m (2¼ yd) white muslin
Wire flowers and foliage in bunches with 22 gauge wires and cover with stem binding tape (pages 24-25). Wire pomegranates with 18 gauge wires (pages 24-25).

1 *Place muslin inside container and drape heavily around sides but keep flat on bottom. Place foam on top and cover with moss.*

2 *Cut green canes into 10 cm (4 in) pieces. Tape cane pieces to bottom of candles (page 23). Group candles centrally.*

3 *Position dried material leaving at least 7.5 cm (3 in) of candle visible.*

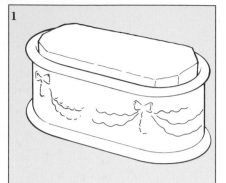

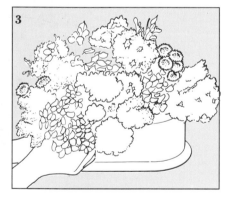

1 *Cut a dry foam block in half, trim and push into container; make sure it fits tightly. Cover with moss and tape in place.*

2 *Position 8 bunches – 2-3 in the centre and the remainder around edge – to create the arrangement's basic shape.*

3 *Intersperse hydrangea heads making them slightly shorter than the other bunches. Add remainder of flowers.*

◄ *Dimension is added to this arrangement by lowering the height of the hydrangea heads in relation to the other flowers.*

You will need:
2 bunches Ambrosinia
2 bunches scabious
20 stems large headed roses
8 stems yellow kangaroo paws
4 heads hydrangea
Wire bunches of flowers with 22 gauge stem wires and cover with stem binding tape (pages 24-25).

► *A pastel-shaded arrangement for a side or occasional table. Fill a glass container with sphagnum moss, then place a piece of foam on top and tape in place. Follow the instructions on page 61, but aim for a more solid, domed shape.*

You will need:
3 bunches artificial berries
2 bunches lavender
1 bunch Achillea
1 bunch marjoram
30 stems peach roses ('Gerdo')
3 heads hydrangea

Summer

Summertime offers a profusion of beautiful blooms for drying and combining to create stunning arrangements. Make an empty fireplace a focal point with a dramatic firescreen, or decorate a plain wall with a posy of pickings. Alternatively, bring a breath of summer into a tired winter interior with a rustic pot of sunflowers or a pair of dazzling yellow topiaries.

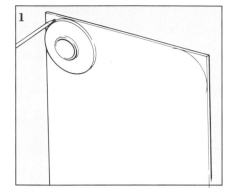

1 Round off corners of wood by drawing around a plate. Cut along pencil line with a saw.

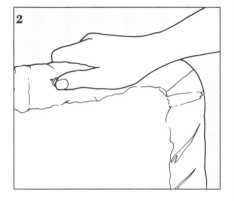

2 Place wood on fabric and trim excess leaving a 5 cm (2 in) border. Fold border over screen edge and pin or glue.

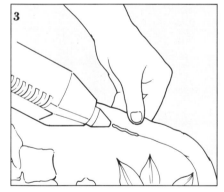

3 Encase cord in a 7.5-cm (3-in) wide fabric strip the length of screen's perimeter. Glue rough edges of piping to screen back and piping to screen front.

◀ *This firescreen is easily decorated with a variety of colourful flowerheads and artificial fruits – simply glue them to the fabric. The fabric strip for the piping can be made from short strips of fabric sewn together end to end to form one long strip.*

You will need:
A piece of plywood approximately 60 x 45 cm (2 x 1½ ft)
Assorted dried flowerheads and artificial fruits
2 m (2⅔ yd) heavy green fabric
3 m (3⅓ yd) x 3.75 cm (1½ in) wide thick cord

▶ *This is a facing, flat-backed arrangement to be viewed from the front and sides only. It is therefore an ideal arrangement to fill the gaping hole of an empty fireplace during the summer months. Soften the front of the display by bending the flowers forwards over the edge of the container.*

You will need:
4 bunches cream zinnias
4 bunches Ambrosinia
4 bunches assorted roses
3 bunches globe thistles (Echinops)
2 bunches sunflowers
14 small heads hydrangea

Wire about a third of flowers onto green canes and cover with stem binding tape (pages 24-25). Wire remainder with 18 gauge wires and bind with tape.

1 *Push foam into container to fit tightly leaving 10 cm (4 in) visible above pot rim. Cover with moss.*

2 *Create the basic shape with some of the taller items at back and shorter flowers around edge.*

3 *To judge the required length of an item on a green cane, measure it against pot before trimming. Position remaining flowers.*

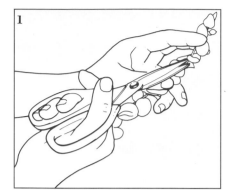

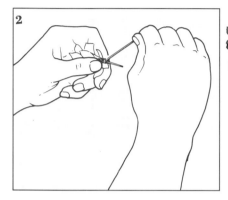

1 *Cut the stems of* Eucalyptus *into short lengths taking care to cut the stems as close as possible to the next set of leaves. This enables the whole stem to be used, not just the top.*

2 *Wire bunches of 3* Eucalyptus *pieces tightly together with 22 gauge wire. Cut off excess wire to leave a clear 5 cm (2 in) of stem. Make the topiary base (page 26) with the branches and either a foam ball or oval shape. Push the* Eucalyptus *bunches into the foam as close together as posible. Cover the quick-drying plaster with a little moss.*

◀ *An unusual foliage topiary.* Eucalpytus *is attractive both for its silver blue-green colour and its interesting leaf formation.*

You will need:
3 branches 2.5 cm (1 in) in
    diameter, 25 cm (10 in) in length
8 bunches glycerined Eucalyptus
A little bung or lychin moss

▶ *A pot full of zest! Fill a terracotta pot with foam and cover lightly with moss. Tape or pin in place (page 19). Wire bunches of Solidago, Celosia and button chrysanthemums with 22 gauge stem wires and bind with stem binding tape (pages 24-25). The remaining flowers can be left on their original stems.*

You will need:
2 bunches Celosia
2 bunches yellow button
  chrysanthemums
  2 bunches Solidago
  10 red roses ('Jaguar')
  6 dark pink peonies
  6 sunflowers
  4 zinnias
  2 m (2¼ yd) wire-edged
  green ribbon

Sunflowers have so much drama, why not preserve their beauty to admire throughout the year. Fill a terracotta pot with foam, cover with moss and pin in place (page 19). Trim sunflower stems to the required length and create a basic framework for the arrangement with a couple of stems at the centre back and a couple either side. Then fill inbetween with other stems. Do not strip the stems of leaves - their twisted shapes break up the solidity of the arrangment.

Moss topiaries can be made in a variety of sizes and shapes. Foam blocks can be cut into different shapes and glued together to form a rounded oblong shape instead of using a foam ball (page 26).

You will need:
3-6 narrow branches or twigs
    approximately 27.5 cm (11 in)
    in length
Bung moss
A little lychin or sphagnum moss

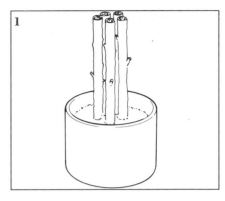

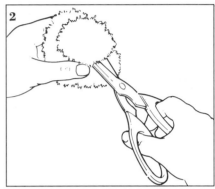

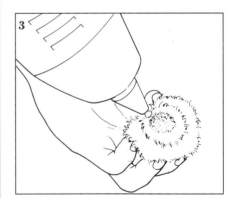

1 *Make a topiary base (page 26) – the branches should extend 20 cm (8 in) above pot rim. Attach foam ball.*

2 *Trim off the root part of the bung moss clumps (page 26).*

3 *Squeeze glue from a glue gun onto underside of moss. Place clumps onto foam as close together as possible. Keep fingers away from hot glue. Cover cement with moss.*

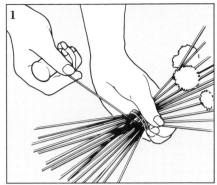

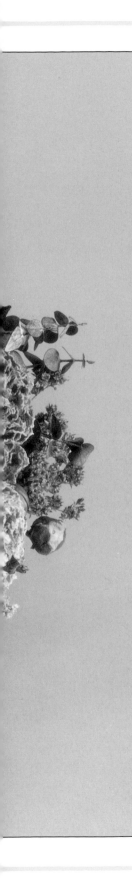

◀ *You will need:*
3 bunches cat mint
2 bunches marjoram
2 bunches glycerined Eucalyptus
30 assorted roses
10 pink peonies
10 heads hydrangea
Cat mint, roses and marjoram are wired in bunches (pages 24-25). Use longer lengths of Eucalyptus*, either wired singly or in pairs.*

▲ *A bouquet of sumptuous summer pickings which can be hung on a wall or door for all to admire.*

You will need:
2 bunches marjoram
2 bunches Ageratum
1 bunch green golden rod
1 bunch Achillea
20 roses

7 peonies
3 heads hydrangea
1 m (1⅛ yd) x 30 cm (12 in) wide silk
Wire 2 peonies singly and 5 small bunches of flowers (pages 24-25). Cover with stem binding tape (page 25).

1 *Gather up a few stems at a time in one hand and wire together just below hand. Continue adding stems, reducing length of extending stems. Secure with wire.*

2 *Make a bow from silk (pages 20-21) and wire to front of bunch.*

3 *Add wired stems and bunches above bow to give fullness, bending forward slightly.*

◀ *A Caribbean cocktail of flowers dramatically set off by the deep blue fabric. Line the basket with the latter, laying it flat on the bottom, but draping around the sides. Then add foam and cover with moss. Create your basic shape with wired bunches of blue larkspur (pages 24-25).*

You will need:
3 bunches blue larkspur
2 bunches yellow button
  chrysanthemums
1 bunch Celosia
1 bunch Carthamus
40 stems red roses ('Jaguar')
7 pink peonies
7 zinnias
2 heads hydrangea

▶ *These dazzling topiaries will bring summer cheer to the home at any time of year. Hair spray will prevent these rather delicate flowers from dropping.*

You will need:
  2 birch poles 7.5 cm (3 in)
    in diameter, 20 cm (8
    in) in length
  12 bunches cluster-flowered
    Helichrysum
A little bung moss

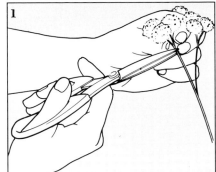

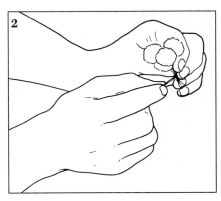

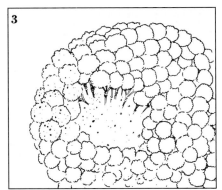

1 *Make 2 topiary bases (page 26). Attach a half foam block to each pole. Take one stem of Santolina at a time and trim off heads leaving 2.5 cm (1 in) of stem.*

2 *Wire heads into bunches of 3-4 (pages 24-25).*

3 *Insert bunches into foam as close together as possible. Cover plaster with moss, then spray flowers with hair spray.*

Autumn

The warm tones and mellow shades of autumn are fully exploited in the following designs. Table centrepieces, decorations for walls and doors as well as topiaries feature fiery red chilli peppers, plump and glossy artificial fruits, rich ruby-red glycerined magnolia leaves and the subtle mauve, blue and green hues of the hydrangea.

You will need:
7 bunches red marigolds
2 bunches red peppercorns
1 bunch cones
1 bunch Ageratum
1 bunch roses ('Minuet')
20 chillies

▼ *This arrangement is truly red hot! Wire the peppercorns, Ageratum, roses and marigolds in bunches (pages 24-25). Wire cones and chillies singly. The latter usually have short stems on which to attach the wire (page 35). Make sure that the chillies extend beyond the other elements to create an interesting, spikey outline.*

▶ *Aim for a long, low shape in this arrangement. It would make an excellent centrepiece for a refectory or trestle table - perhaps for a harvest-time or Thanksgiving feast.*

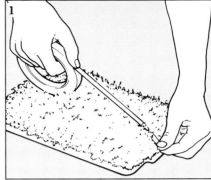

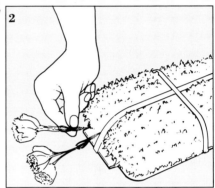

You will need:
5 bunches artificial grapes
1 bunch Ambrosinia
36 assorted roses
35-40 poppy seedheads
9 stems artificial berries
5 stems white paper flowers

Wire flowers with 22 gauge stem wires; artificial grapes with 18 gauge wires (pages 24-25). Cover with stem binding tape (page 25). Leave artificial berries and white paper flowers on original stems.

1 *Cut a block of foam in half to create a shallow full-width piece. Place on a black plastic tray and cover lightly with moss. Tape moss and foam to tray.*

2 *Insert flowers into sides of foam at either end of base. Add berries – 2 at each end, one shorter than the other, 2 along each side and 3 on top of the foam. Fill in with remaining material.*

Autumn

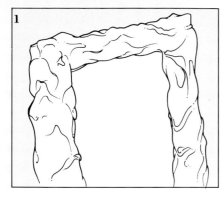

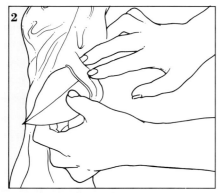

You will need:
1 wooden-framed mirror
40-50 red-dyed magnolia leaves
36 sunflowers
3 m (3⅓ yd) fabric

1 Drape fabric around mirror frame and glue in place once a good shape has been achieved.

2 Cut bases of some of magnolia leaves, apply glue and insert into fabric folds. Group other magnolia leaves and glue onto fabric at intervals. Cut sunflowers from stems as close as possible to the heads. Place at intervals around the frame, some in groups, and glue in place when satisfied with arrangement. Add a few sunflower leaves to lighten the effect.

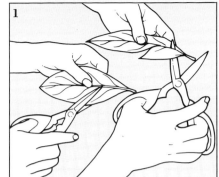

◀ *You can transform any plain wooden-framed mirror in this way. Adapt the colour scheme to coordinate with your interior decor by using alternative flowers and fabric.*

▶ *A spectacular topiary destined to be the focal point of any interior. Choose a luxurious fabric in a rich colour for the base.*

You will need:
A branch 7.5 cm (3 in) in
    diameter, 45 cm (18 in) in length
Thin branches of contorted
    willow
A large quantity of glycerined
    magnolia leaves
Bung moss
1 m (1⅛ yd) fabric
Make a topiary base setting the
trunk and twigs in plaster (page
26). Attach foam ball to top, cover
in wire netting and wire to trunk.

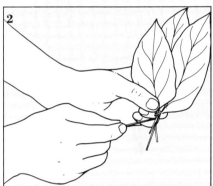

1 *Magnolia leaves come in serveral different sizes. Choose medium-sized leaves. Cut larger leaves to size by trimming the side of the leaf leaving enough stem to wire.*

2 *Hold leaves in groups of 3, splayed slightly at the top. Wire together using 22 gauge wires (pages 24-25). Push into foam ball starting at the top. The right sides of leaves should face inwards. Keep turning topiary while adding bunches of leaves. When complete, wrap pot in fabric tucking raw edges into pot. Cover inside of pot with moss.*

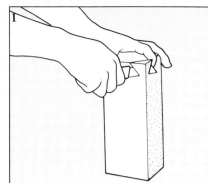

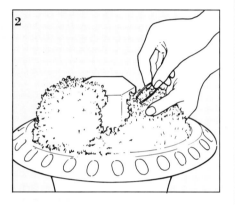

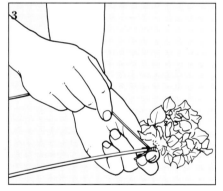

1 *Push foam blocks into urn to fill. The middle block should be approximately 5 cm (2 in) higher than others. Cut off top corners using a craft knife.*

2 *Cover foam lightly with moss and pin in place (page 19).*

3 *Place first hydrangea in centre, then a few each side. Fill inbetween with rest of canes. Add wired heads around edge and bend over urn rim.*

◀ *This arrangement is most effective when different varieties and colours of hydrangea are used in combination.*

You will need:
40 assorted hydrangea heads – 60-70 heads for an all-round arrangement
Wire all except 3-4 hydrangea heads onto green canes; wire remainder with 18 gauge wires (pages 24-25). Bind with brown stem binding tape (page 25).

▶ *You will need approximately 50 hydrangea heads to make this large-scale topiary. Follow the instructions on page 26 to make the topiary base. Insert the trimmed stems of the hydrangea heads into the foam to cover. Cover the plaster in the container with bung moss.*

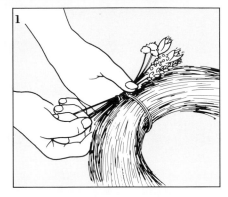

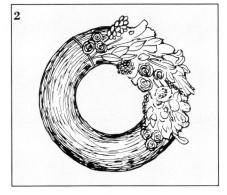

1 *Bind an 18 gauge wire with stem binding tape and attach to ring for hanging (page 23). Wire woodland drieds into bunches of 3 and bind with tape (page 25). Cut Eucalyptus into 10-12.5 cm (4-5 in) long pieces. Cut proteas from stems leaving 7.5 cm (3 in) of stem. Tie end of a length of green garden twine to ring for binding on stems.*

2 *Place a few stems of Eucalyptus onto ring and bind tightly with twine keeping it taught at all times. Add a couple of proteas, bind tightly then add a woodland bunch. Bind tightly once more. Continue until ring is covered. Make 9 small double-looped bows and 1 large bow for the top (pages 20-21). Insert bows into wreath at intervals.*

◀ *Wire-edged ribbon is excellent for dried flower arranging in that it can be creatively shaped and will remain so.*

You will need:
A straw ring 35 cm (14 in) in
    diameter
5 bunches assorted dried
    woodland items, eg cones, tree
    mushrooms etc
2 bunches dried Eucalyptus
12 proteas
4-5 m (4½-5½ yd) wire-edged
    ribbon

▶ *This magnificient wall plaque makes an original interior decoration. It could be hung horizontally in a suitable location for extra drama.*

You will need:
2 bunches dried grasses
2 bunches morrison
2 bunches glycerined Eucalyptus
1 bunch red species roses
26-30 glycerined magnolia leaves
9 proteas
4 sunflowers
1 string chillies
Wire magnolia leaves in groups of
3 and Eucalyptus in groups of 5-6
with 22 gauge wires (pages 24-
25). Wire grasses and morrison
into small bunches. Cover all wires
with stem binding tape (page 25).
Proteas and sunflowers can
remain on original stems.

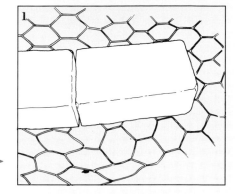

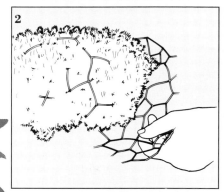

1 *To make plaque base, cut foam blocks in half to form 2 shallow pieces. Cut a strip of wire netting slightly longer than 3-4 foam blocks end to end and wide enough to wrap around width of one block.*

2 *Lay wire netting flat and cover lightly with moss. Place blocks onto moss end to end. Bring sides of netting into meet middle top of foam. Twist cut ends of wire together. Make sure netting is tight around foam; if not, tighten at this stage. Cover underside of plaque with plastic (page 20). Attach an 18 gauge wire covered in stem binding tape to the top for hanging (page 23).*

You will need:
9 asssorted roses
6 zinnias
3 m (3⅓ yd) ribbon
Fabric to line basket

▲ *Use a piece of silk or satin to line a wire basket. Trim the excess fabric around the rim and using a glue gun, glue the fabric to the rim. Glue the ribbon around the rim to cover, making loops in the ribbon as you work. If the basket is oval, make sure that the ribbon ends meet at one flatter side of the basket. Glue on flowerheads in a group, and a matching group on the opposite side of the basket. Additionally, you could make roses from scraps of the lining fabric by folding and gluing to hold. Intersperse these amongst the dried flowerheads.*

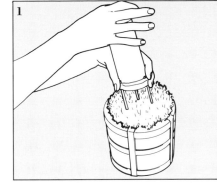

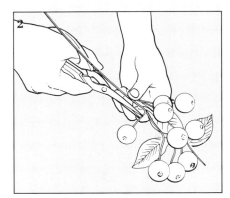

You will need:
6 stems small assorted artificial
  fruits
5 artichokes
3 stems large assorted artificial
  fruits
3 open poly-dried roses
1 candle
If the artificial fruit stem is hand
wrapped, it is best to unravel the
wrapping. In this case you will
have long enough wires on the
undivided fruits not to have to
wire them up.

1 *Cut foam block in half and push
into pot. Trim corners if too big.
Cover lightly in moss and pin in
place (page 19). Cut a green cane
into 3 pieces and tape to bottom of
candle (page 23). Place centrally.*

2 *Cut artificial fruits off stems
retaining wire stem. Wire large
singly; small in groups of 3 or 5
(pages 24-25). Place artichokes,
fruits then roses.*

Winter

Enhance your home in winter with arrangements that are rich and varied in texture whilst subtle in colour combinations. Here we have pots of fragrant herbs to grace the kitchen, a lychin-covered photograph frame that would make a memorable gift and a taste of winter woodland in a natural display of leaves, cones and grasses.

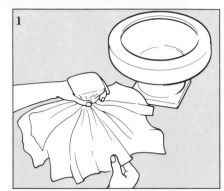

1 Wrap footed bowl in velvet, wire around neck of bowl (page 19) and cover with ribbon.

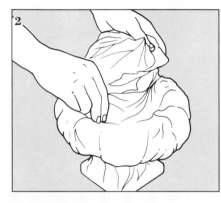

2 Turn pot upright and tuck excess fabric into top of pot.

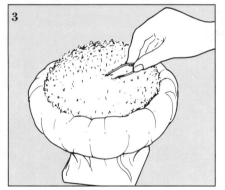

3 Push foam into bowl to fit tightly, cover with moss and pin in place (page 19). Wire cones and fruit of one stem (pages 24-25 and 97). Other material can remain on original stems.

You will need:
2 bunches open cones
1 bunch dry Eucalyptus
1 bunch small cones
3 stems artificial poly-dried peonies
3 stems artificial poly-dried roses
3 stems artificial fruits
3 stems artificial grapes
½ m (½ yd) red velvet
½ m (½ yd) red paper ribbon

▲ Aim for a fairly solid, high-domed shape when positioning the flowers. Then intersperse the fruits and cones, and lastly the Eucalyptus to lighten the arrangement.

▶ The colour and texture of the container is important here, and its roughly-hewn solidity balances the confusion of woodland drieds.

You will need:
4 bunches assorted woodland cones
2 bunches grasses
1 bunch glycerined beech
5 stems artificial fruits

◀ Bring a warm glow to your winter table with this small beeswax candle arrangement. Fill the container with foam, cover with moss and pin or tape in place (page 19). Insert pieces of green cane into the bottom of the candles (page 23) and group in the centre of the foam. Wire dried items in bunches (pages 24-25), and group to make a 'collar' around the candles, bending the lower bunches well down over the container's edge.

You will need:
2 bunches woodland cones
1 bunch green marjoram
1 bunch marjoram
20 stems red species roses ('Nikita')
20 stems yellow roses ('Golden Times')
6 narrow beeswax candles

▶ A charming, compact arrangement suitable for a bedside table. The lavender heads should break out slightly from the otherwise smooth outline.

Winter

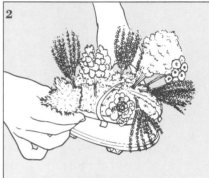

You will need:
2 bunches Queen Anne's lace or
   cow parsley
1 bunch lavender
1 bunch purple clover
30 assorted roses
2 heads artificial hydrangea
1 stem blue Delphinium

1 Place small piece of foam into
container, cover with moss and
tape in place. Wire small bunches
of Queen Anne's lace, lavender,
roses, clover and Delphinium with
22 gauge wires (pages 24-25).
Cut each hydrangea head into 5
pieces. Wire each with 22 gauge
wire (pages 24-25). Bind all stems
with stem binding tape (page 25).
Position about 6 lavender bunches
to create basic shape.

2 Fill in with remainder of flowers
pushing them deeper into foam, if
necessary, to make shorter than
lavender.

◀ *A commonplace frame for a special family photograph can be immeasurably enhanced by gluing on dried tree lychins. They perfectly echo the yellowing tonal qualities of an ageing black and white photograph.*

▶ *A winter extravaganza! Pack the bunches of drieds close together to achieve a solid arrangement with a smooth outline.*

You will need:
5 bunches Helichrysum
4 bunches Anaphalis *(pearl everlasting)*
4 bunches red zinnias
3 bunches blue thistles
3 bunches Celosia
3 bunches peach roses
2 bunches red roses
12 heads hydrangea
8 stems artificial fruits
Fill container with foam so that it fits tightly. Shave off corners with a craft knife. Cover lightly with moss.

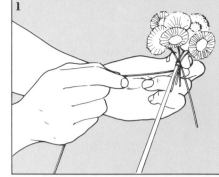

1 *Wire about 80% of ingredients in groups onto green canes (pages 24-25). Cut fruit from stems (page 97) and wire onto green canes in groups of 3. Wire the remaining material in groups with 18 gauge stem wires (pages 24-25). Cover all wires with stem binding tape (page 25).*

2 *Using 5 items on green canes, create basic shape, ie first bunch in centre top, the other 4 between centre and sides. Position the wired bunches around edge of container. Bend forwards slightly to soften hard edge of pot. Fill in framework with remainder of material on canes.*

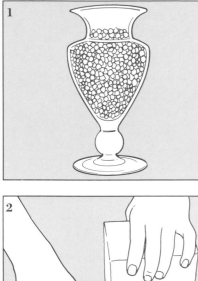

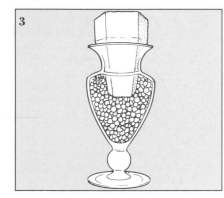

1 *Fill vase up to its neck with hydrangea florets.*

2 *Cut approximately three-quarters of a foam block in half lengthways. Cut off bottom corners.*

3 *Foam should fit tightly into vase neck leaving 7.5 cm (3 in) above rim. Fill to rim with florets pushing down sides of foam with round-ended knife.*

◄ *This arrangement should not be attempted until you are quite confident since the piece of foam is very slender and will begin to disintegrate if stems are repeatedly inserted and removed.*

You will need:
2 bunches green marjoram
2 bunches glycerined Eucalyptus
2 bunches Agastache mexicana
2 bunches dahlias
40 stems dark pink roses
8 stems artificial fruits
4 heads hydrangea
Hydrangea florets
Wire flowers in bunches with 18 gauge wires (pages 24-25); wire hydrangea heads singly. Cut fruits off original stems and wire with 18 gauge wires in groups of 3 (page 97). Cover all wires with stem binding tape (page 25).

► *To make this spectacular lavender urn, place a block of foam into the container making sure that at least half of the block is above the pot rim. Round off corners. Divide each lavender bunch into 4 and trim stems to 10-12.5 cm (4-5 in) in length. Wire with 22 gauge wires and bind with stem binding tape (pages 24-25). Place the first bunches at the top of the foam and work downwards keeping the bunches tightly packed.*

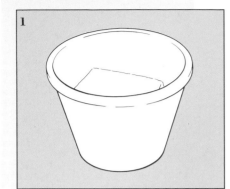

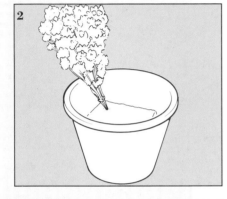

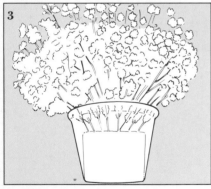

▶ *These rustic pots of herbs would make an attractive display in a country kitchen. Group them together and raise one or two pots on split logs, terracotta tiles or bricks to give varying heights. Instructions for making the bay balls are given on page 23.*

You will need:
5 bunches dried marjoram
1 large bunch fresh rosemary
1 large bunch fresh bay
Wire marjoram and rosemary in bunches onto stem wires and cover with stem binding tape (pages 24-25). Bay can be left on original stems.

1 *Cut foam block to fill pots a half to three-quarters full. It should fit tightly.*

2 *Insert bunches one at a time into foam until packed – each herb in a separate pot.*

3 *The low level of foam helps to create the upright nature of the arrangements. Place bay and rosemary pots in a warm, dry place for a week or so.*

Christmas

Dried flowers and seedheads, cones and nuts, cinnamon sticks and artificial fruits can be arranged together to produce a rich array of decorations for the Christmas and New Year celebrations. The following pages feature unique gift wrapping, advent rings of traditional red and gold or cool green and silver, seasonal topiaries that provide a stylish alternative to the usual tree, a magnificent candelabra adorned with fruit and roses, and finally a grand garland for a festive fireplace.

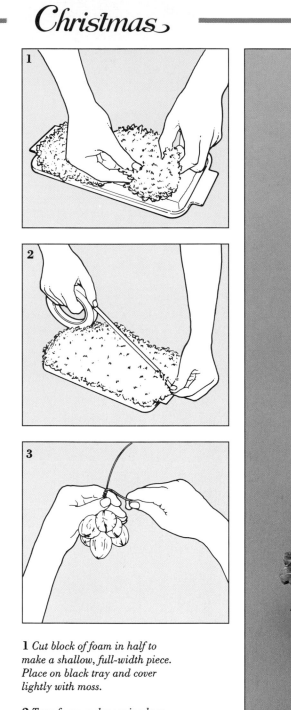

1 *Cut block of foam in half to make a shallow, full-width piece. Place on black tray and cover lightly with moss.*

2 *Tape foam and moss in place. Cut 2 green canes into 6 pieces. Insert 3 pieces into the bottom of each candle (page 23).*

3 *Wire cones with 22 gauge wires (page 25). Mount walnuts onto wires (page 25) and wire together in groups of 5.*

◀ *A traditional centrepiece for the festive table. Beeswax candles give off a sweet, honey-like scent when lit.*

You will need:
11 bunches walnuts
25 assorted cones, one half sprayed gold
2 beeswax candles

▲ *Make your Christmas gift packages highly individual and stylish by gluing on nuts, decorative miniature baubles, dried or paper flowers and pumpkin seeds. Glycerined roses (page 16) look sumptuous against a luxury fabric giftwrap. Trail lines of glue over the fabric and sprinkle with glitter. Shake off excess.*

Christmas

◄ As an unusual alternative to the traditional Christmas tree, why not make an elegant moss topiary which can be decorated with miniature baubles. Follow the instructions on page 26 to make the topiary base, but use a foam cone in place of the ball. Refer to the instructions on page 81 for applying the moss. Glue baubles onto moss to complete. You could make two matching trees to stand either side of a fireplace.

► A chunky topiary of plump, glossy artificial fruits which would make a colourful and original table centrepiece for a festive feast.

You will need:
A branch approximately 7.5 cm
    (3 in) in diameter, 20cm (8 in)
    in length
100 small artificial fruits
36 large artificial fruits

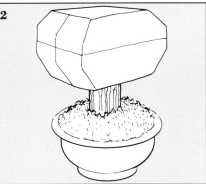

1 *Set the branch in a bowl using nylon-reinforced plaster (page 26). Cover top of plaster with moss.*

2 *Trim the ends of obling pieces of foam at an angle and glue together to form a large oblong oval shape (page 26). Mount onto branch. Cut fruits from original stems leaving as much stem as possible. Wire large fruits singly with 18 gauge wires; smaller fruits in small and large bunches (pages 24-25). Cover all wires with stem binding tape (pages 25). Position fruits close together in foam. Intersperse artificial leaves.*

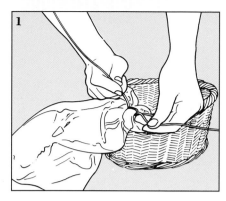

▼ *If you wish to fill the basket with pot pourri, line the basket with fabric before you begin.*

You will need:
5 bunches large cinnamon sticks
Approximately 20 cones
1 m (1⅛ yd) fabric
1 m (1⅛ yd) ribbon

1 *Attach fabric to basket rim at 15 cm (6 in) intervals with 22 gauge wires.*

2 *Mount cones onto 18 gauge wires (page 25). Spray with gold paint. Wire bunches of cinnamon together (page 25).*

3 *Attach cinnamon bundles and cones to basket rim with wire 'stems'. Trim excess wires. Tie ribbon around each cinnamon bundle to cover wire.*

▶ *You will need:*
A 30 cm (12 in) diameter foam ring
4 bunches gold grapes
4 bunches lavender
3 bunches marjoram
2 bunches woodland cones
  touched with gold paint
20-25 stems small red roses

2 stems artificial plums
4 candles and candleholders
2 m (2¼ yd) ribbon
Wire lavender and marjoram in very small bunches with 22 gauge wires (pages 24-25); wire cones. Cover all wires with stem binding tape (page 25).

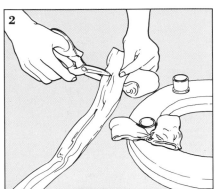

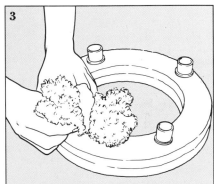

1 *Position candleholders at equal distances around ring, pushing bases into foam.*

2 *Cut ribbon into 8 equal lengths and make single loop bows without tails (pages 20-21). Place 2 bows by each candleholder.*

3 *Mount candles, then position cones. Add lavender, then marjoram and roses. Complete with plums and gold grapes.*

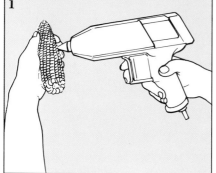

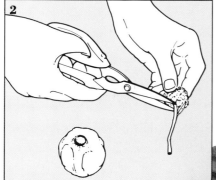

You will need:
A twig wreath 35 cm (14 in) in
*   diameter*
Assorted dried cones
Assorted artificial and dried fruits
Walnuts
3 dried corn cobs
1 m (1⅛ yd) ribbon
Cover an 18 gauge wire with stem
binding tape and twist onto
wreath for hanging (page 23).

1 *Apply a line of glue from a glue*
gun down the length of corn cobs.
Attach at intervals to the wreath.

2 *Trim any stem from*
pomegranates and other fruits as
close to fruit as possible. Glue the
larger items to wreath. Fill in with
small items until wreath is full
and chunky. Remember to leave
space at top for bow. Make a large
double-looped bow and tie onto
wreath (pages 20-21).

◄ *An unusual yuletide door wreath. It is best to check the position of your items before gluing since they cannot be easily moved once glued.*

▶ *A truly elegant Advent ring. Position candleholders and mount candles. Spray the cones with silver paint and wire (page 25). Wire Eucalyptus in bunches and group around the candles. Add cones and fruits. Finally, add the paper flowers to give highlights.*

You will need:
A foam ring 30 cm (12 in) in
*   diameter*
3 bunches glycerined Eucalyptus
3 stems white paper flowers
3 stems artificial green plums
18 cones
4 candleholders and candles

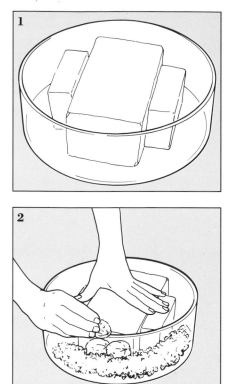

1 *Place blocks of foam into dish leaving approximately a 2.5 cm (1 in) margin in which to fit the nuts and moss.*

2 *Place nuts and moss around foam both to hold foam in place and to look attractive.*

3 *Tape cane pieces to bottom of candles (page 23) and place 1 cm (½ in) apart. In order, add hawthorn, fruits, cinnamon. Pin chilli string to foam (page 19).*

◀ *A highly original candle arrangement which would make a spectacular decoration for a New Year celebration.*

You will need:
1 bunch cinnamon sticks
10 walnuts
8 lychin-covered hawthorn twigs
5 open pods
4 stems artificial fruits
String of round chillies
Lychin moss
3 assorted church candles
Wire hawthorn with 18 gauge wires. Cut fruits from original stems and wire in small bunches (pages 24-25). Cinnamon sticks should be wired singly with 22 gauge wires.

▶ *An extravagant candelabra display for a grand festive gathering. The rich colours of the fruit combine dramatically with the deep red roses. Remember not to leave the arrangement unattended when the candles are lit.*

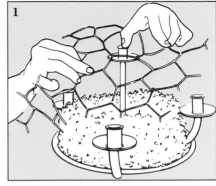

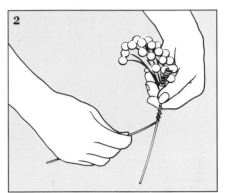

You will need:
21 bunches artificial grapes
15 bunches chillies
40 red roses
10 stems assorted artificial fruits
4 candles

1 *Place foam blocks on top and bottom levels of candelabra and cover lightly with moss. Cut a circular piece of wire netting and place over foam on top level. Cut a second circle of wire netting, make a cut halfway to the centre and fit around centre stem of candelabra to cover foam. Wire netting securely to edges of 'shelves'.*

2 *Wire roses into groups of 3, chillies in groups of 3-9 and bunches of grapes singly (pages 24-25 and 35). Trim fruits from original stems (page 97) and wire in groups. Position the grapes first, then fruits, roses and finally chillies.*

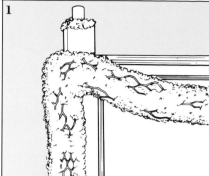

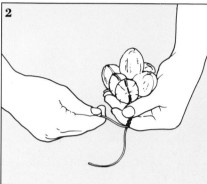

You will need:
4 terracotta pots
11 bunches gold grapes
5 bunches cinnamon sticks
130-150 walnuts
100 stems red roses
24 cones, 12 sprayed gold
15 woodland cones
12 artificial plums
Lychin and sphagnum moss
5 m (5½ yd) velvet

▶ *Complete this dramatic fireplace display by tying ribbon around the cinnamon bundles so that it covers the wire, and add a large double-looped bow to the centre point of the swag (pages 20-21).*

1 *Make a moss rope (page 20) to form a swag along front of mantelpiece and 'tails' either side. Secure in place with nails or by threading wire through back of mantelpiece. Twist fabric loosely around tube beginning in centre and working outwards. Wire in place at ends of tube. Fill pots with foam and wire with 18 gauge stem wires (page 23). Push wires through moss rope to netting on far side and twist onto wire.*

2 *Mount nuts onto wire stems (page 25) and wire together in large bunches. Fill pots with walnuts and roses. Wire fruits in groups of 3-4, bunches of grapes singly, cinnamon sticks in bunches (pages 24-25) and cones. Wire onto rope, interspersed with clumps of lychin moss.*

DEDICATION

To my wonderful children, Olivia and Clarence,
who make everything worthwhile.

AUTHOR'S ACKNOWLEDGEMENTS

Topher Faulkner, Hannah Catling, Cherry Clark, Caroline Little,
Angela Chamberlain, Vanessa Lee, Sarah Eastwood, Donna Henderson, Francis Bearman
and Jo Finnis without whom none of this would have been possible.
Dried flowers: *Robson Whatley, R & R Flowers, Machin & Henry, Tudor Rose*;
silk flowers: *Best Blooms, H Andreas, Austin & Co, Forever Flowers*;
sundries: *Cocquerels* and *Peter Harvey*.

All products used in this book are available from Veevers Carter Flowers,
125 Sydney Street, London SW3, tel: 071 370 0549.

CREDITS

Editorial: Jo Finnis
Design: Alison Jewell
Photography: Steve Tanner
Photographic Direction: Nigel Duffield; Jo Finnis
Illustration: Geoff Denney Associates
Typesetting: Julie Smith
Production: Ruth Arthur; Sally Connolly; Neil Randles
Director of Production: Gerald Hughes